STREET SMARTS

STREET SMARTS

TRUST YOUR INSTINCTS,

OUTSMART DANGER,

AND STAY SAFE IN

A WORLD THAT ISN'T

DANNAH EVE

WILLIAM MORROW
An Imprint of HarperCollins*Publishers*

Some names and identifying details have been changed to protect the privacy of the individuals involved. The people whose stories appear within these chapters have granted their permission to share them.

Without limiting the exclusive rights of any author, contributor or the publisher of this publication, any unauthorized use of this publication to train generative artificial intelligence (AI) technologies is expressly prohibited. HarperCollins also exercise their rights under Article 4(3) of the Digital Single Market Directive 2019/790 and expressly reserve this publication from the text and data mining exception.

STREET SMARTS. Copyright © 2026 by Dannah Eve. All rights reserved. Printed in the United States of America. No part of this book may be used or reproduced in any manner whatsoever without written permission except in the case of brief quotations embodied in critical articles and reviews. For information, address HarperCollins Publishers, 195 Broadway, New York, NY 10007. In Europe, HarperCollins Publishers, Macken House, 39/40 Mayor Street Upper, Dublin 1, D01 C9W8, Ireland.

HarperCollins books may be purchased for educational, business, or sales promotional use. For information, please email the Special Markets Department at SPsales@harpercollins.com.

hc.com

FIRST EDITION

Designed by Elina Cohen
Illustrations by Alexis Seabrook

Library of Congress Cataloging-in-Publication Data has been applied for.

ISBN 978-0-06-343888-0

25 26 27 28 29 LBC 5 4 3 2 1

My professor turned mentor turned family. Chuck, you weren't just a teacher or a guide, you became a cornerstone in my life.

Even with a career as decorated as yours—from serving as a Secret Service agent, public defender, and chief deputy district attorney to teaching and inspiring countless students—your brilliance was matched only by your heart. You taught me that kindness is strength, integrity is nonnegotiable, and humor can brighten even the hardest days.

Though you are deeply missed, your legacy lives on in all the lives you touched, especially mine.

Contents

Introduction: Why Me, and Why You Need This Book — ix

1. Trust Your Gut: Intuition and the Psychology of Survival — 1

2. Lie to Survive: How Minor Mistruths Can Help Keep You Safe — 13

3. Buckle Up: Your Guide to Safe Driving — 33

4. Swipe Smart: The New Rules of Dating Safely — 59

5. Squad Safety: Going Out While Staying Safe — 71

6. Workplace Well-Being: Surviving in Your Office — 85

7. Flying Solo: How to Rock Living on Your Own — 101

8. Adventures in Traveling Alone: How to Jet-Set Safely — 117

CONTENTS

9. Campus Chronicles: Navigating College Life — 143

10. Stay Cyber-Smart: Protecting Yourself in the Digital Jungle — 159

11. Mass Violence: What to Do when the Unthinkable Happens — 181

Conclusion — 197

Acknowledgments — 201

A List of Safety Tools — 207

Index — 213

Introduction

Why Me, and Why You Need This Book

Ever since I was a child, I've had an extreme sense of awareness of the intricacies of the world around me. Though my devoted parents helped nurture my sense of street smarts, it also seemed somewhat innate. I had a natural ability to discern both safe and not-so-safe situations as they arose, and I sensed what I could do to protect myself when difficult predicaments popped up.

This heightened sense of my surroundings, and instinct for what needed to be done to navigate the world safely as a girl, carried me through many tough moments as I grew up. One of the hardest came when I was around ten years old on a beautiful spring afternoon that forever changed my sense of safety in the world.

It was a Friday, my favorite day of the week, and I was about to walk home from school with a group of friends for the very first time, after days of begging my mom for this bit of freedom. But as the school bell rang, a wave of anxiety washed over me—our group had shrunk from eight to just three. I had no means of contacting my parents (kids didn't have cell phones then), and I grew more and more anxious as we walked. My nervousness spiraled into flat-out fear when I noticed a suspicious van creeping behind us. I suggested we change our route, but the van kept following our every move.

When my friends left for their own houses, I found myself alone, and my sense of danger intensified. The van suddenly sped up, and a man opened the passenger's door. Without thinking, I threw my backpack into a bush and ran. Rounding the corner to the main street I was aiming for, I spotted my neighbor and her dog. In desperation, I called out the dog's name: "BJ!!" The neighbor stopped in her tracks as I rushed over, surely as white as a ghost. The last image I recall from that day—one that remains etched into my memory—was the furious expressions of the creepy men in that van.

My interest in street smarts and crime prevention later turned into a passion for criminology. When I was preparing to graduate from high school, I had no idea what I wanted to pursue in college. But my eyes lit up when I saw that criminology was a top option at my school, the University of Nevada, Las Vegas (I later moved on to the University of New Mexico in Albuquerque). I'd always been fascinated by true crime, and I soon decided my chosen path: Go to Quantico and become an FBI special agent.

In August 2010, I walked into my very first crime class and was immediately obsessed with it. Some of the other college classes I was most excited by were Sociology of Law, Forensic Anthropology, Abnormal Behavior, Social Psychology, and Causes of Crime and Delinquency. Four years later, I was set to graduate with summa cum laude honors. Along the way, I was lucky enough to rub shoulders with many special agents from the Secret Service, ATF, DEA, FBI, you name it. This was all thanks to one much-beloved professor with a highly decorated career in the Secret Service.

Charles "Chuck" Barth, my late mentor, was like family to me; he had a colossal impact on the course of my life. Starting in the 1970s, Chuck became a Secret Service agent in the New York field office, where he protected Pope John Paul II, Fidel Castro, Israeli prime minister Menachem Begin, and Presidents Gerald Ford, Jimmy Carter, and Richard Nixon. He went on to become an assistant US attorney and, later, chief deputy district attorney. I took multiple college courses with Chuck; his nickname for me was "D," and he had this magic ability to sense whenever I was going through a tough time. He'd call me over to his desk after class and let me talk, vent, and cry about whatever challenging situation I might be going through, whether it was personal, academic, or athletic. He always had my back, and I can't credit him enough for all the unfailing support and guidance he offered me.

I was lucky enough to know Chuck for almost ten years before unexpectedly losing him. At age sixty-seven, on Christmas Day 2020, he underwent a heart procedure during which everything seemed to go wrong, and he tragically passed away in early January. The last time I was able to give Chuck a big hug was at my wedding in 2018, and my parents thanked him for always being there for me.

Now, you're probably wondering about what happened with my planned FBI stint. Well, it didn't happen—I never went to Quantico. Two weeks before graduating, I met Chuck for lunch to talk about my career path and next steps. He offered to make any calls he could to help me land my dream job. We discussed the many opportunities out there, as well as the heaviness that goes hand in hand with a career as a Fed. He painted a very vivid picture of what my life could look like, including the darker realities.

I reflected on my conversation with Chuck that day and ultimately chose a different path for two reasons. One is that my mentor recognized—and celebrated—my sensitivity and big heart, and he worried that even though I could have the career of a lifetime as a federal agent, I'd never be able to go home at the end of a long day and let go of what I'd experienced. The horrific things you see, hear, and face head-on in such a challenging profession become the kinds of traumatic memories you can't shut off at the end of the day, and Chuck knew that I would struggle with that part of the job. I ultimately didn't want to sacrifice my mental health and well-being for a career.

The second reason is that I'd never fully wrapped my head around the fact that being a mom and a special agent might not easily go hand in hand, at least not for me. I had always known I wanted to have a family, and I'm sure plenty of female FBI agents successfully manage this kind of double life, but I just couldn't envision it for myself. Plus, if I weren't able to turn off the hardest parts of my job when it was just me on my own, how would I be able to do it while juggling motherhood and attempting to raise a tiny human?

I hadn't thought at length about how my choice in career might play into my desire for a family, and after talking with Chuck, I started putting some dots together for myself. He didn't discourage me from pursuing my dreams; instead, he helped me understand the sacrifices involved. I realized the career path I'd chosen just wasn't what was best for me, and I made peace with that.

Instead, I stepped back into something I'd known and loved my whole life, beginning a career centered on fitness and soccer. Still, as the years rolled by, I felt a bit alienated and empty when I thought of my hard-won criminology and psychology degree, which was kind of . . . languishing, if not outright going to waste.

In 2022, two large-scale tragedies served as a catalyst for everything I do today. The first was the Fourth of July parade shooting in Highland Park, Illinois—my hometown. My son had just been born in June, and my family decided to skip the parade; we were on the tail end of the COVID-19 pandemic, and it was just too risky to bring my newborn son to such a highly populated event. But many people I loved attended the parade that sunny day, and they were traumatized for life by what they experienced.

On the morning of the shooting, I sat in the bliss of my newborn bubble . . . until my dad called and I could hear in his voice that something was deeply wrong. A mass shooting, he said.

Almost everyone we knew went to that parade each year. It was a local tradition. I quickly called a friend, who was hysterical. She'd been in the direct line of fire and tried to describe the chaos that was unfolding around her. She'd seen people shot right in front of her; the ground was littered with bodies.

I could barely comprehend what I was hearing. The location where the shooter had perched was right above a store where my mom and I had regularly shopped when I was growing up. It was all too much. The realization that something like this could happen anytime, anywhere—even in my hometown—hit me deeply. Plus, I was a new mom, so the whole tragedy hit differently. I remember nursing my son with tears streaming down my face.

The second incident that woke me up was 2022's highly publicized Idaho case in which a young man murdered four promising college students, robbing them of their lives and futures.

After both senseless tragedies, my new-mama heart lay awake, incessantly pounding all night, because I couldn't get the faces of the victims or their heartbroken families out of my head.

After another sleepless night fixating on these events, I suddenly experienced an urge rise within me. It felt like a calling to do *something*, anything, to help prevent more people from suffering the way all those victims had. In short, I wanted to help—and in that moment I realized I might have the perfect way to do it. I decided to start a project to spread accessible safety tips to people everywhere and, just maybe, save a life. Putting this project online was the quickest and easiest way to share my ideas as broadly as possible.

And so my Street Smart Blonde social media accounts were born. In a matter of a few months, my following grew to 50,000, then 200,000, 300,000, and into the millions. I've received hundreds of heartfelt messages from complete strangers sharing stories of how they believe my advice helped save their lives—from knowing exactly what to do when being followed to escaping a scary situation when cornered by a store employee.

When I took to social media to share my tips, I didn't know the impact they would have. The advice I've included and expanded on in this book is the material that hit home the hardest with my online community, including information on living alone, dating safely, traveling, and employing practical safety tips that can be applied on a day-to-day basis. These tips are the bread and butter of how to live aware but not in fear; they're strategies to help empower you in your day-to-day life.

I hope you, the reader, will come away from this book feeling strong and validated in the knowledge that there are active measures you can take to protect yourself and avoid becoming an easy target. While you can't control fate—or the people around you—you can take measures to stay safe. It's not about being afraid; it's about taking the simple precautions discussed in these pages and being ready to use them when necessary.

We live in a complicated and often scary world. But here's the good news: We don't have to take it lying down. There are simple ways we can prevent crime, and there are skills we can learn to help ourselves stay safe, whether it's during a mass shooting, while on a date, when traveling solo, or when doing everyday errands, like getting gas. It's not just about learning individual tips—it's about carrying a safety-conscious mindset with you wherever you are. You'll be protecting not only yourself but your family, friends, and wider community as well.

The one thing that would make life even sweeter? If I could pick up the phone and tell Chuck all about it. He'd be so proud of me. Instead, I'll relish the knowledge that this book has the potential to help you in your day-to-day life. Getting this book into as many hands as possible is one of my biggest goals, so after you read this, feel free to pay it forward and share what you've learned with your loved ones.

I hope you begin to experience your own sense of empowerment while you're reading this book and processing its message. I want nothing more than a safer world for women (and everyone else too!). Reading and using the advice in this book could be the first step toward that reality.

Trust Your Gut

Intuition and the Psychology of Survival

Psychology plays a real role in why crime happens, how it happens, and who perpetrates it, but fortunately psychology also plays a part in preventing it. My aim with this book is to give you insight into the psychology of criminal behavior, reveal the power of intuition, and amp up your street smarts so that you can approach life with a good balance of caution and self-confidence. My hope is to trigger your natural survival instincts, helping you trust, believe, and *act* anytime you have a feeling that something isn't quite right.

I often say, "Live aware, not in fear," but as author and security expert Gavin de Becker says, fear is a gift—a gift that serves to protect us from violence. Having a better understanding of the role that psychology plays in both criminal behavior and its prevention allows us to trust our intuition as a way of life.

The Reality of Crime: What the Data Tell Us

A 2024 social media trend asked women, "Would you rather be left alone in the woods with a man or a bear?" The overwhelming majority of women chose the bear. This result may have surprised men, but it came as no shock to women, who feel the need to constantly assess their safety. It's a burden that many men would never consider.

Don't Blame the Victim

> Society often places blame on women for the crimes that are committed against them. Let me be clear: There is *never* a situation in which appearance, attire, type of employment, or other factor gives anyone the right to blame the victim for a crime that was inflicted on them. The responsibility lies solely with the perpetrator. *Full stop.*

According to the most recent FBI statistics compiled in the Uniform Crime Reporting Program, crimes involving categories of sexual assault are overwhelmingly committed by a man victimizing a woman. The most recent five-year (2018–2023) trend shows that 85.78 percent of rape offenders are men, with 89.51 percent of their victims being female. Though women are obviously capable of committing sexually related violent crimes too, stats show that the bulk of them are committed by men against women.

While these statistics provide important context, I don't want this knowledge to put you in a perpetual state of panic or unease. It's just the unfortunate reality that women are at a disadvantage. This is due not only to our physiological makeup but also the systemic conditioning that makes it harder for us to act on our intuition for fear of being accused of overreaction or paranoia. Our "nice girl" training can be hard to override.

The Danger of Denial

Denial—a false peace of mind that crime "won't happen to me"—is a dangerous mindset that can put you in unnecessary danger. The best way to combat the real risk of violence is to understand that it doesn't discriminate and that it can happen to anyone, anywhere. But here's the good news: Knowledge empowers you. Don't put your head in the sand. Living aware is the best way to protect yourself.

The Psychology Behind Intuition

Crime and violence typically don't happen out of thin air. They tend to follow patterns that are preceded by subtle warning signs. Learning to read those signs and lean into the feeling that something is off can grant you the necessary time to react accordingly and remove yourself from a threat. You must learn to follow your intuition and trust your gut feelings, which can help you detect red flags (such as shifts in body language, tone of voice, or manipulation tactics) that our rational mind may try to dismiss—and can even save your life. (Of course, practicing listening to your intuition will also help you in every aspect of your life, not just with regard to personal safety.)

Though our intuition may not always be 100 percent correct, it's an evolutionary survival instinct that gives us the capability to preempt danger, and it's there for a reason. Wouldn't you rather take decisive action and be ever so slightly embarrassed if it turns out you're wrong than ignore a warning and end up fighting for your life?

Although intuition is an innate human ability, lots of women aren't used to channeling it. That's okay—once you've developed that little voice in the back of your head and learn to trust it, it will become stronger and more powerful.

Learning to Trust Your Gut

Learning how to trust your gut is something you can practice in all kinds of situations, not just potentially dangerous ones. Start honing your instincts on life's more mundane circumstances. Does that job offer really feel perfect, or could it be slightly too good to be true? Do you and your new work friend really have a lot in common, or are you bonding out of shared frustration with your boss? Learn to listen to your inner voice by trusting it with small decisions. The more confidence you have in it, the more likely you are to respond well in a tricky situation.

Let's say you're on a first date and the person insists on driving you home afterward. The date was fine, but something about the way he pushed the idea of driving you home left you uneasy; you couldn't shake that gut feeling. That's your intuition speaking, and you need to listen to it. Ignoring that instinct could mean isolating yourself with someone whose true intentions are suddenly, and dangerously, revealed—intentions your intuition warned you about, even when your logical mind didn't recognize them. Anytime you feel that something is "off," it's crucial that you stop to consider that feeling—and be prepared to act on it.

Decoding Red Flags

When you notice red flags, it's important to look at them in context. A "good" person might occasionally make a mistake, but what matters is how they respond when they realize they've crossed a line; one red flag doesn't *always* mean trouble. Pay attention to whether they take responsibility and work to make you feel comfortable. A trustworthy person should step back and respect your boundaries, but you'll still want to proceed with eyes wide open.

Behavioral Warning Signs

Criminals aiming to gain the trust of their intended victims often use specific, psychologically rooted behaviors and tactics. These warning signals and manipulation strategies can vary depending on what the person is trying to achieve, but they're always red flags we need to learn to detect. Let's break down some of the behaviors and tactics that should set off your internal warning bells:

- **EXCESSIVE CHARM.** If lavish flattery, love-bombing, fixating on making you feel special, or showering you with random gifts seems too soon and too good to be true, it probably is.

- **THE INTERVIEWER.** Criminals will sometimes conduct an "interview" to test their potential target and feel them out before committing a crime. This is a way of determining how easy of a target you might be. Often these interviews are disguised in a way that makes the questions sound harmless.

Some examples: "I love morning runs when I'm all by myself, don't you?" or "Do you live with roommates or are you Miss Independent?"

- **FAST-TRACKING RELATIONSHIPS.** Expressing intense emotions super early in a relationship (e.g., professing their love or saying something like "I've never felt so close to a person this quickly"), rushing intimacy, pushing for exclusivity or a relationship title, or taking excessive interest in your hobbies or taste in music, sports, or restaurants are all reasons to hit pause.

- **PUSHING BOUNDARIES.** Boundary pushing takes many forms: showing up unexpectedly or uninvited, subtly testing your limits by asking for small favors or making slightly inappropriate jokes to see how you respond, and casually invading your personal space to test your level of discomfort, all while slowly establishing dominance or control.

- **FALSE ASSURANCES.** Also known as fake promises, this is a common tactic used to manipulate, disarm your suspicion, or gain your trust. Example: Someone says, "I promise I'll come over for just one drink"—and then, hours later, you still can't get the person to leave.

- **INSULT MANIPULATION.** This type of emotional manipulation is a psychological tactic that often takes the form of baiting you with a passive-aggressive insult. It's meant to destabilize your sense of self-worth and make you second-guess yourself. For example, "Wow, you're actually pretty smart." This isn't flirting; it's actually a red flag and a possible power move.

Script It Out

Disclaimer: In a perfect world, "No" would be a complete sentence. But when said by women, it's often looked at as "Challenge accepted." Therefore, as you'll soon learn, my Lie to Survive strategy (aka lying to preserve your own safety) can help you escape an uncomfortable or potentially dangerous situation without it escalating.

You're sitting at a bar when a man approaches, sits down next to you, and sparks conversation. Within a brief period of time, he orders two shots and slides one in your direction. You politely decline, to which he responds with a sarcastic laugh, "You don't look like a girl who could handle shots anyway." You immediately start to feel uncomfortable and have a gut feeling that this isn't a conversation you should entertain. Here are three replies you could use to safely exit the situation:

- "Not tonight, I'm driving—thanks, anyway" (as you start walking away). If he tries to convince you to stay or lure you back over, simply smile and keep those feet moving.

- You can look at your phone, pretend you're getting a call, and say, "Thanks, anyway; I'm so sorry, but I have to take this" as you head toward your group of friends (or whomever you're with).

- You can tell him you're sick. Say something like "Sorry, I have diarrhea and need to run to the bathroom right now." Then exit quickly. It might sound ridiculous, but in reality sometimes using a repulsive bodily function as an excuse can save the day.

- **STORY INCONSISTENCIES.** Someone who gives contradictory facts about their life (background, work, and so on), then avoids specifics or changes the topic when asked for clarification, should cause you to hear alarm bells.

- **UNSOLICITED HELP.** Offering you help when it's not necessarily needed—and making it difficult for you to decline—is a tactic that can make you feel uncomfortable and vulnerable.

- **GROOMING.** Trust is built using friendship, mentorship, excessive acts of kindness, and attentiveness, but the intention is eventual exploitation.

- **ISOLATION.** You are encouraged to distance yourself from family, friends, and colleagues in an attempt to isolate you from your support system.

- **GASLIGHTING.** Someone causes you to doubt your perceptions or distorts your reality by lying or denying that certain events or conversations ever happened. Someone might say, "You're the one who started this argument," even though they were the instigator.

- **FEAR AND INTIMIDATION.** Threats, passive-aggressive language, or physical intimidation are used either subtly or overtly to control you or influence your behavior.

- **MANUFACTURING CRISIS.** Fabricating an emergency or injury to elicit sympathy (and your compliance) is a tactic used to get you into a position of unforeseen jeopardy. For example, serial killer Ted Bundy would prey on a woman's instinct to help by presenting himself in a position of false vulnerability—

pretending to use crutches, a cast, or an arm sling to garner his victims' sympathy and get them into his vehicle.

> **FALSE AUTHORITY.** Claiming a position of power or authority (e.g., posing as law enforcement) can make someone seem more credible, allowing them to gain trust and compliance.

> **FLIPPING A SWITCH.** A sudden shift in behavior (we're talking a 180-degree change in personality) triggered by rejection or refusal, in which a "nice guy" suddenly flips a switch and turns vulgar, violent, or outraged, is *always* cause for concern . . . and *always* a hard pass. Walk (safely) away.

Real-World Safety Story

It was my last day of work, so five of us went out for dinner and then to a local club. Among the group was a guy called Andy, who was a store manager, and a guy called Dan, who had worked at the shop only for a few days.

While we were at the club, Andy let me know that he liked me. I had no idea he felt this way and tried to let him down as gently as possible. His mood changed, and I started feeling quite nervous around him.

Andy was our designated driver that night. I was concerned about getting into his car, but I assumed it would be okay because I would be the first one to be dropped off.

Unfortunately, Andy went in the opposite direction, meaning that I would be the last one dropped off. He was driving like a maniac, speeding and racing around corners. He dropped off two of our group, leaving me in the passenger seat and Dan sitting behind me. As he pulled into Dan's street, I told Andy that I was getting out at Dan's house (who I'd only known for a few days). When he stopped, I managed to get my door open, but Andy grabbed ahold of my arm and wouldn't let me leave. Dan was outside the car and grabbed my other arm to try to pull me out of the car. Fortunately, I'd managed to undo my seat belt, and with Dan's help I was able to get out of the car, and Andy drove off.

—Alison

THE TAKEAWAY

Never isolate yourself with someone who makes you feel uncomfortable or unsafe. Trust your gut!

Dreams as a Survival Tool

Your dreams are part of your intuition; don't disregard any dream that might seem relevant to a current or future scenario. Dreams can reflect a subconscious recognition of past experiences, thoughts, and feelings, allowing us to discern patterns in our current situations. In other words, they could be your survival instincts speaking. Although dreams can't necessarily predict future events, they can awaken our deepest instincts and serve as a reflection of our darkest concerns.

If you awaken from a dream that leaves you uneasy, consider these questions:

- Are there any red flags in your personal life that you've ignored?

- Is there someone in your life who makes you feel uncomfortable?

- Are there any upcoming events that don't feel right?

A real-world example of paying attention to your dreams could be something like this: Every day on your way to work, you stop at your local coffee shop for your morning Joe. A newer male barista that has seemed very friendly (in a harmless way) suddenly mentions a rare record that he's been keeping an eye out for. You don't think anything of it. That night, you wake up from a dream with your heart pounding. In your dream, the barista has broken into your apartment and is playing music on your record player. When you wake, you notice that the record he mentioned is the same one that you were recently gifted, which happens to be sitting on your coffee table (and is visible from the sidewalk outside). Coincidence? It's anyone's guess, but your intuition is likely picking up on something your rational brain might try to dismiss. It's enough to warrant a red flag for Mr. Barista.

In life, there's no "right" way to get through, to survive. And sadly, there's no manual for every single situation you might find yourself in; each moment that arises is unique to you. The best thing you can do to protect yourself and stay safe is to heed your instincts and intuition. *You* are the only one who can evaluate your surroundings and recognize any feelings of fear, apprehensiveness, uneasiness, or confusion. You're also the only one who can properly recognize the complexity of a given set of circumstances in your life—you're the person going through this specific scenario in this specific moment. In one instance, it may be best to play along with a prospective attacker to save your life; in another, it may be best to fight like hell (I'll go into more detail on both of these courses of action later in the book).

Trust yourself. Your intuition is one of the few things in life that *always* has your back.

Lie to Survive

How Minor Mistruths Can Help Keep You Safe

Spoiler alert: I am 100 percent in support of lying if it helps protect your personal safety. I've been practicing this my whole life; my parents instilled this skill in me. So please don't feel guilty for doing it! It's a wonderful first line of defense and can help save you from an uncomfortable or potentially dangerous situation.

Lying doesn't come naturally to most people. Sure, we may tell a few harmless lies here and there to protect people's feelings ("I love that dress on you!"). But it's drummed into us that society values truthfulness, and therefore some women may be conditioned to feel uncomfortable lying, even when their safety depends on it.

Before we dive in, I want to share the origin story behind Lie to Survive, because this strategy isn't just something I teach—it's something I've lived. When I was a young kid, my parents and I had games we played on road trips. My mom's parents lived about four hours away, which meant we had plenty of time to play them. One of those games we called the "lying game." Another was the "what if" game, which is similar and one I talk about more on page 25. My parents would throw out different scenarios in which I was the main character, and my job was to think fast—come up with a story, a lie, to get myself out safely. These games were fun. We laughed a lot while playing, but at the same time, I was learning how to think on my feet and navigate difficult situations.

It became a road trip tradition. They'd ask things like "What would you say if a stranger at the park asked you for help or asked if you were alone? Now, what would you say if a man with a puppy told you he had more in his car and wanted to give you one?" The more we played the lying game, the quicker I got. It became second nature.

As I got older, I started using this skill in the real world, and it proved invaluable. Whether it was navigating an uncomfortable conversation, defusing a tense situation before it escalated, or finding a way to let someone down gently without confrontation, lying to survive became a tool I could rely on. It wasn't just about safety—it was about control, confidence, and knowing how to handle unpredictable moments on my own terms. I didn't have a name for it back then, but the instinct stuck with me.

Years later, as an adult, I decided to share this strategy with the world. But let's be honest—"lying for your safety" isn't the most compelling phrase. Around that same time, I was deep in my *Formula 1: Drive to Survive* era (a docuseries on Netflix —huge F1 fan over here), and I kept thinking, "What flows with 'lie'?" Then one night, it clicked—Lie to Survive! And just like that, it had a name. What started as a road trip game is now helping people around the world. This concept isn't new; deception has been a pivotal survival tool for millennia. But turning it into something simple, memorable, and easy to apply? That's something you can carry with you for life.

Remember . . . Your safety comes before anyone else's feelings.

Refuting the "Lying Isn't Nice" Lie

Over the years, I've received many messages from women saying they find lying morally questionable because of how they were raised, or they simply feel uncomfortable lying because it doesn't come easily to them. As women, we need to get past the idea that we owe it to be transparent to others. We're taught to smile, act polite, tell the truth, and never hurt anyone's feelings. This might sound good in theory, but it's actually damaging advice when it comes to surviving and thriving in the real world, where strategic lying is a valuable tool for women.

I am a truthful person to my family and friends, but I *will* pretend I'm waiting for my husband if a strange man approaches me when I'm at a restaurant alone . . . and so should you. Without any guilt.

Just the Facts

Nearly one in two women in the United States have reported "unwanted sexual contact victimization" at some point in her life.[*]

The social focus on telling the truth, no matter what, makes us beholden to pleasing other people at our own expense. There are tons of great people out there who deserve honesty, but there are also creeps (or *potential* creeps) who don't deserve either our

---

[*] Kathleen C. Basile, Sharon G. Smith, Marcie-jo Kresnow, Srijana Khatiwada, and Ruth W. Leemis, *The National Intimate Partner and Sexual Violence Survey: 2016/2017 Report on Sexual Violence* (National Center for Injury Prevention and Control, Centers for Disease Control and Prevention, 2022).

presence or our truth. People who disrespect personal boundaries and set off our internal alarms deserve whatever concocted fiction is needed to get away unscathed.

Because we can't always sniff out ill intentions, it can be hard to know if someone trying to buy you a drink at a bar is a decent person or a shadier sort. This is why it's important to protect yourself until they prove themselves to be trustworthy. What is your intuition telling you? Your best bet is trusting your initial gut feeling, as well as playing it safe and staying in well-populated areas. You never want to isolate yourself with someone you just met.

I'll never forget the time I was in Mexico on spring break in my senior year of high school. I went with my cousin and a bunch of his guy friends whom I grew up with. We had a rule within the group that if I was creeped out by someone, I would go over to one of the guys and put my arm around them, and they would pretend I was their girlfriend (this rule also applied to them if they needed to be "saved" from a woman who was hitting on them).

On this trip, we were out at a club one night when I noticed a weird, drunk older guy in his forties checking me out. I was all of seventeen and not remotely interested in being the focus of this man's attention. When I realized he was following me (he had already trailed me toward the women's restroom), I headed back around to the front of the bar, made a beeline for one of my guy friends, and leaned up against him. Though the man still approached me and tried to buy me a drink, he eventually got the hint and realized I was "with" someone (he obviously had no clue my faux boyfriend was just a good buddy).

The average man is physically stronger than the average woman, and we need to take this into account when dealing with strangers. Having a man around (or a "pretend" man around—more on that later) helps scare off creeps like Mexico Guy, because to get to you the creep must contend with the dude by your side, or the one who's supposedly en route, which means you're no longer the "easy" target. Don't appear to be one.

➤

Below are a few common scenarios in which I'd suggest you lie to survive. After each example, I'll provide a lie you can give in response.

The most important takeaway here? You're trying to show you are not alone, that you have a male figure either with you, on his way to meet you, or at the location where you're heading. Think of these responses as a jumping-off point—you can adjust them to fit your situation and needs, but keep the motive in mind.

Disclaimer: If it becomes clear that your "story" has been compromised . . .

Consider this all you need as "proof" that your gut was correct; you need to get out of there. Lying to survive is just your first line of defense. If your cover is blown, you must switch up your approach. At this point, your safety is all that matters, so just do whatever you need to remove yourself from the situation. There's nothing embarrassing about asking for help. If you're freaked out, ask the bartender or security guard to walk you out to your car, or call a guy friend to walk you home. But never leave alone. If you need to call 911 for help, do it. Remember, your safety comes before anyone else's feelings.

You're reading or studying in a coffee shop . . .

. . . and a strange man approaches your table to ask what you're reading. After a bit of seemingly harmless chit-chat, he asks, "Are you here alone?"

You: "No, I'm waiting for my boyfriend. He'll be here soon."

The why: Being alone makes you an easy target—so never act like you're alone, even if you are. No matter what, you're always waiting for someone: a boyfriend, husband, guy friend, your dad, or your brother. Saying "he'll be here any minute" lets the stranger know that you won't be alone for much longer and there's an "intimidating" male figure who knows your exact whereabouts.

You're sitting at a bar, waiting on a friend . . .

. . . when a man sidles up beside you, says hi, and asks, "Can I buy you a drink?"

You: "I'm flattered, but I'm good, thanks. My husband [or boyfriend] is on his way. He's right around the corner."

The why: It's iffy to accept a drink from a stranger, no matter how "nice" they may seem. Never let your guard down. Remember, alcohol can only cloud your judgment and leave you more vulnerable. Using the "my husband is coming" excuse lets him know that you're not easy prey, and often this is enough to cause the person in question to give up and walk away.

If the person persists and you start feeling uncomfortable . . .

Try accepting the drink, but don't drink it; or "accidentally" spill it, then get up and go to the restroom to clean up, call for backup, or simply leave (if it's safe to do so). You could also tell the man that you aren't drinking that night because you're driving.

Don't become agitated or confrontational. It's imperative to keep your cool and remain even-keeled in situations like this.

Growing confrontational can trigger the individual and cause the situation to escalate. You want to get away from this person without drama (or worse), so it's best to feign niceness even if you're feeling freaked out. Lie to survive! Remember?

Order the Angel Shot

If someone at a bar keeps bothering you, ask the bartender for an "angel shot"—most bartenders know this is code for "I need help" and will come to your aid.

You're heading home in an Uber . . .

. . . when your driver starts making casual chit-chat. It's all fine and dandy until they ask you if you're heading home (or to your AirbnB, your hotel, or some other location where you might be staying).

You: "No, I don't live here. I'm just heading to my brother's house for a surprise party."

The why: It's not smart to give out your home address to a stranger. Letting the driver know where you live could make you an easy target in the future. You can avoid this conundrum by having the driver drop you off a block (or even a few doors down) from your home, assuming it's a safe area to walk the rest of the way. Simply change the address when you enter your destination in the app. Also, telling the driver you're staying with your brother indicates that there will be a man in the picture soon.

If you're being held captive or in a domestic violence situation . . .

. . . try asking your attacker if you can order pizza, then call 911 and pretend to order one. Say, "I'd like to order a pizza."

Dispatcher: "Did you mean to call 911?"

You: "Yes, I'd like to order a large pepperoni pizza to be delivered to 007 Street Smarts Lane. Is it big enough for three people?"

Dispatcher: "We'll send help over right away."

The why: In 2019, an Ohio woman made a similar 911 call to signify that she was in a domestic violence situation. This was quick thinking on her part; the dispatcher identified the threat and sent help to her house. Making a call like this can be a discreet way to request immediate help without alerting the aggressor.

If you're in a potentially dangerous situation with an abuser or attacker in a hotel room . . .

. . . tell the person you'd like to order room service. Then call 911 and ask whether you've reached room service.

Dispatcher: "No, this is emergency services. Did you mean to call us?"

You: "Yes, I'm in room 312 and I'd like to order a bottle of wine." (If you call from a landline (the hotel phone), which you'd typically order room service from, the dispatcher should automatically have your address.)

The why: This is a straightforward way to contact emergency personnel before a situation reaches full-crisis mode.

You're in an elevator with a stranger . . .

. . . and they ask if you live in the building.

You: "No, I'm just visiting my boyfriend."

The why: Again, it's always best to pretend you're visiting a male figure, even if you do live in the building in question. Never give someone clues—either directly or indirectly—about where you live!

A Quick Guide to Elevator Safety

- If you don't like the vibe of a person who's already on the elevator, don't get on; wait for the next one.
- Locate the emergency call button as soon as you get on the elevator.
- If you must enter an elevator with someone you're unsure of, or you feel even mildly uneasy about them, wait for them to push their floor button first. If they ask you what floor you're going to, give them a different floor number than the one you live on or are actually heading to.
- If you start feeling really creeped out, act like you forgot something ("Oh, I need to jump out—I forgot something") and get off the elevator immediately. Don't forget, lie to survive. You can also head back down to the lobby.
- You can Facetime a friend or pretend to go live on social media—having witnesses should help deter the person from doing anything overtly sketchy.

- If the person in the elevator says they're going to the same floor as you, say something like, "Oops, I'm actually on three."
- If you get off on your floor and someone follows you, never go to your room. Instead, you can hover around and pretend to make a call, saying something like "Hey, I'm outside, which room is yours?" You could also get back on the elevator and go down to the lobby.
- If the person on the elevator keeps staring at you or making you uncomfortable and you feel like tackling the situation in a more head-on way, face them and say "hello" in a firm tone with strong eye contact. This isn't an invitation for a conversation, it shows assertiveness and that you're watching them. Depending on where you are in the world, saying "hello" might not be customary; if that's the case, or if you simply don't feel comfortable speaking, you can make firm eye contact and nod. Be mindful of your posture and demeanor; you want to give the sense that you're not an easy target. Don't ever turn your back to them or you could give them a good vantage point.

You're at your university or local college haunt . . .

. . . and someone asks if you go to school there.

You: "Nah, I'm just here visiting my dad. He works here."

The why: You get it by now—you never want to reveal where you live. Saying your dad works at the school gives you an easy explanation for being on campus (or nearby) without revealing too much about yourself. You could also say you're visiting your boyfriend or brother.

Script It Out

WORLD TRAVEL EDITION

You're traveling alone through Europe on a solo backpacking adventure. The tour guide on your Florence bus trip strikes up a conversation. He asks you questions like where you're from, if you're traveling alone, and where you're staying.

You: "I'm from [anywhere but your actual home city]. I'm traveling with a group of friends, but they're on a different tour today. We're staying with my uncle, a couple towns over."

Tour guide: "Ah, beautiful. What's your uncle's name? I might know him; I know everyone within a hundred miles of here."

You: "Ricky. I doubt you know him—he just moved here recently."

Tour guide: "Okay. What are your plans for tomorrow?"

You: "I have another tour with my friends [in a town you're not planning to visit]."

Of course you can talk to people on your travels. In fact, traveling would be much less fun if you didn't—part of the joy of seeing new places is encountering new people. But you need to stay safe and protected while doing so. Telling some harmless lies when meeting new people doesn't make you a bad person; it makes you a smart one. Don't trust people who haven't earned your trust. Telling the tour guide you're from a different city in your home country makes sense, as does misrepresenting who you're traveling with and where you're staying. Remember, you're not lying for fun, you're lying to ensure your safety.

Why "No" May Not Be the Way to Go

One of the biggest comments I get on my social media accounts is " 'No' is a complete sentence." People tell me that women shouldn't *have* to lie to protect themselves. Of course simply saying no *should* be enough to get a sketchy man to leave us alone. But not all men will take no for an answer. This is why lying to survive is your friend. Telling a man no will sometimes serve only to anger him, prompting potential escalation, which is obviously the last thing you want. When you're feeling scared or uneasy or just don't want to engage for some reason, don't just tell someone no or say "leave me alone"; come up with a concrete reason for why you can't or won't do the thing they're asking you to do, even if that reason is fictional.

Fight, Flight, Freeze, or Fawn

When facing a perceived threat, there are four primary stress responses that might happen to you. All these reactions are normal; they are reactions from your sympathetic nervous system, designed to keep you alive in moments of high stress and danger. The response you experience will depend on your physiology and previous experience as well as on the situation and the intensity of the perceived threat.

- **FIGHT.** When you're in fight mode, lying to survive is irrelevant. You're literally prepared to fight your attacker or the perceived threat; in this heightened state, you'll want to confront the threat aggressively, head-on. Your body will prepare itself for a fight and adrenaline will kick in. You might feel a wave of intense anger and an urge to hit, kick, punch, or stomp. If you're in a situation like this where you're fighting for your life, be as loud as possible and try to draw as much attention to yourself as you can. Screaming specifics—"Rape!" or "He's trying to kill me!"—is more effective than simply yelling "Help!" or "Call 911!"

- **FLIGHT.** In flight mode, your primary instinct will be to flee the scene. The rush of adrenaline will compel you to get away from the perceived threat immediately, whether this is running or quickly hatching an escape plan. If possible, your best bet is always to get as far away from danger as possible, but sadly this is not always feasible—sometimes another survival instinct might kick into gear.

- **FREEZE.** Freezing is actually fight-or-flight on hold. The fancy name for freezing is attentive immobility or reactive immobility. In this mode, your body will seem to shut down and go quiet as it prepares for danger. Some people take longer to process danger than others; they become like a deer in headlights. You might feel a sense of dread and feel your heart beating loudly. This freeze response may occur when fighting and fleeing aren't options. Generally, this is an involuntary survival response.

  So how can you prepare if you know you tend to freeze in an emergency situation? Play the "what if" game—one of the games I used to play on road trips with my parents. This game is one of the most effective mental exercises to help prepare for real-world safety scenarios. It's a simple but powerful way to train your mind to stay alert and responsive in moments where people tend to panic or freeze. The concept is exactly what it sounds like—you run through possible "what if" situations in your head: *What if I noticed someone following me while I was walking to my car at night? What if someone approached me while I was at an ATM? What if I was in an*

Uber and the driver started driving in the wrong direction? Think about your escape options in these hypothetical situations, so if you ever find yourself in an actual one, you'll be better able to overcome your freeze response and act accordingly. Playing this game with yourself will make you more prepared and confident in your ability to keep yourself safe.

- **FAWN.** Fawning is often a subconscious last resort that kicks in when fighting, fleeing, or freezing either didn't work or weren't feasible options. Sometimes fawning can be as simple as "playing nice" and letting a creepy guy down easy, but it can also be used as a conscious tactic to survive a dangerous situation. Your body may be assessing the danger and realizing that if you don't play along, the person could attack you or even kill you. When you fawn as a response to a perceived threat, you're choosing to go along with your attacker; you're playing along to protect yourself. This is a form of lying to survive. In these situations, you'll need to do *anything you can* to stay alive. The fawn response is sometimes used by those trapped in domestic violence or abuse situations or by people who are threatened by a violent attacker. Bottom line: Do whatever you have to do, and say whatever you have to say, to escape with your life.

The Art of Surviving: When Playing Along Is Your Only Option

Sometimes survival comes down to a choice no one should have to make: Play along, or risk it all. It's a gut-wrenching reality that countless people have faced—whether trapped in the grip of a predator, enduring the terror of a serial killer, or living through the unpredictable rage of domestic violence.

The 2023 Netflix film *Woman of the Hour* featured stories of a couple of the women who managed to escape the 1970s *Dating Game* serial killer, Rodney Alcala. One of the victims, the character Amy (who was based on an actual victim of Alcala's), was a teen runaway who went on a day trip with Alcala into the California desert to shoot photographs. He began attacking her, and she woke up bloodied and bruised beside him—staring death in the face in the middle of nowhere. Cornered by Alcala (who she didn't know was a serial killer at this point), she was forced to make the conscious decision to act like everything was okay—the fawn response. She didn't scream. She didn't run. She didn't fight back. Not because she didn't want to, but because he had already been incredibly violent with her, and deep down she knew her only shot at survival was to play his game. Every word she spoke, every move she made, was a calculated lie. Lying wasn't a weakness—it was courage. It was strength. It was brilliant. And she survived.

Real-World Safety Story

> It was a sweltering afternoon in the early 1980s, and I was leaving a shop in a strip mall in Fort Myers when I noticed a man striding toward me across the parking lot. Something about him set off alarm bells in my head. He had a professional-looking camera slung around his neck, and as he got closer, he smiled and said, "I'd love for you to model for me."
>
> Every instinct in my body screamed nope. His tone was too eager, his eyes too intense. I mumbled something noncommittal and turned toward my car, picking up my pace.
>
> Then he started running.
>
> Heart hammering, I sprinted the last few steps, yanked open my car door, and threw myself inside, slamming the lock down just as

he reached me. He grabbed the handle and rattled it violently. "Come on," he pleaded, voice shifting into something almost desperate. "You'd be perfect."

I refused to look at him as I fumbled to start the car. Finally, the engine roared to life, and I tore out of the lot, watching him shrink in my rearview mirror.

When I got home, still shaking, I called the police. They took a report, but I figured that was the end of it.

Years passed. Then one day, out of the blue, I got a call from law enforcement. They had an update.

The man who had chased me? Christopher Wilder, a serial killer. He had murdered several women, including one who had worked for my parents.

I had come within seconds of being another name on that list.

—Jennie

THE TAKEAWAY

Appearances can be deceiving. Even if someone looks normal and seems friendly, you never truly know. If alarm bells go off, lean into it and remember that trusting your gut can save your life.

When Playing Along Saves Lives

Playing along is not giving up; it's buying time. It's about using the tools you have in that moment to stay alive until there's an opportunity to escape or signal for help. Here are a few situations where this strategy has been the difference between life and death:

❭ **SERIAL KILLERS AND PREDATORS.** Elizabeth Smart was kidnapped at knifepoint from her Salt Lake City bedroom in 2002 at age fourteen and held captive and sexually assaulted for nine months by a man named Brian David Mitchell and his wife, Wanda Barzee. She endured unimaginable terror, but she played along to survive. She didn't provoke her captors. "Things that I'd always told myself I'd never do, I would do them if it meant I would survive. If it meant that one day I would be able to go back home and be with my family again, I would do it," she told NBC News' Meredith Vieira in 2013.* She complied just enough to stay alive, while quietly looking for her chance to escape—and eventually she got one. She was rescued by police officers after being spotted out with her captors when she was fifteen.

❭ **DOMESTIC VIOLENCE.** In abusive relationships, victims often "play nice" during volatile situations to avoid triggering more violence. They might seem to agree with their abuser, stay silent, or even apologize for things they didn't do—all while planning how to get out safely.

❭ **ARMED ROBBERIES OR HOSTAGE SITUATIONS.** In moments of chaos, victims who remain calm, comply with demands, and avoid drawing attention to themselves are often the ones who survive. It's about not escalating the situation, but instead waiting for the right moment to seek help.

❭ **HUMAN TRAFFICKING.** Survivors of trafficking often recount how they played along with their captors' demands, building a

---

* Tracey Jarrett, "'I Was Broken Beyond Repair': Elizabeth Smart Recalls Kidnapping Ordeal," NBC News, October 5, 2013, https://www.nbcnews.com/news/us-news/i-was-broken-beyond-repair-elizabeth-smart-recalls-kidnapping-ordeal-flna8c11336267.

false sense of trust to avoid punishment or worse. They used that trust as leverage to create opportunities for escape.

When Is It Better to Not Play Along?

If you're in danger of a perpetrator taking you to a second location, then you should aim to escalate the situation. (If you're taken from your first location, your chances of survival decrease significantly.) For example, you're running alone when two men in a van pull up and try to grab you. In this case, you'll want to kick, yell, hit, bite, scream, and do whatever else you can to get away.

Playing Along Is Strength, Not Weakness

The goal is always to escape to safety, and you must do whatever you need to do to get out alive. If playing along is the only way, you should do so without guilt or shame. Even if it means doing and saying unimaginable things to help yourself survive or escape, do it. Your life is worth it.

Let me be clear: Playing along is not giving up. It's being resourceful enough to know that fighting back in that moment might not work. It's courage under pressure, thinking clearly when everything inside you is screaming to run or fight. To anyone who has ever had to do this or who might find themselves in this position someday, please know: You are not to blame for what someone else did to you. Your survival was an act of bravery.

The Universal Sign for Help

There's a universal sign for help, signaled with a hand gesture, that you can use if you ever feel threatened or unsafe. This gesture entails holding your hand with your thumb tucked into your palm, then folding your remaining four fingers down, trapping your thumb within your fingers. It's meant to be performed a few times at once so it's more easily visible. The Canadian Women's Foundation created this signal in 2020, and it has taken off worldwide thanks to TikTok.

Just as you're always attending to your surroundings to keep yourself safe, be aware of this hand signal and be ready to take action if you see someone else using it.

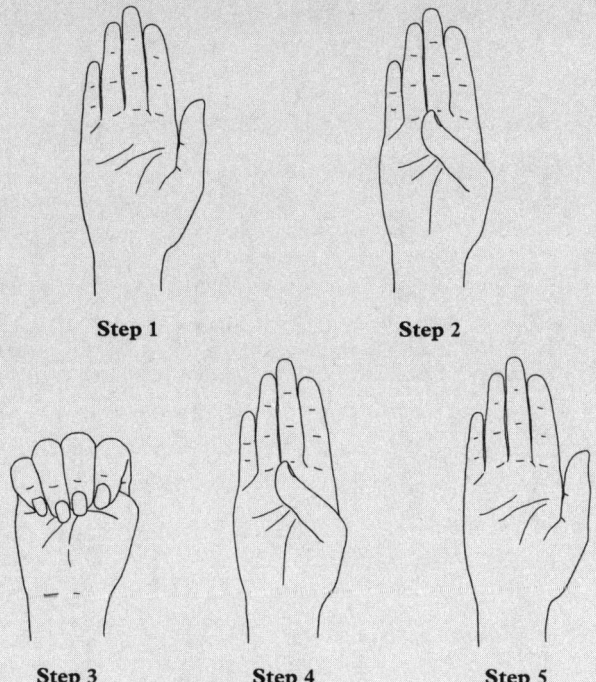

Step 1 Step 2 Step 3 Step 4 Step 5

Buckle Up

Your Guide to Safe Driving

Driving is arguably the riskiest thing most Americans do every day. The following tips can help you stay safe behind the wheel—and they go deeper than simply driving sober and staying on top of your local weather conditions.

Put Your Phone Away

This one may seem obvious, but before you get behind the wheel, put your phone on silent and stash it away. In 2022, more than 3,300 people were killed in accidents because of distracted driving (this includes texting), and an estimated 290,000 people were injured in crashes involving distracted drivers.[*]

---

[*] "NHTSA Launches Put the Phone Away or Pay Campaign; Releases 2023 Fatality Early Estimates," National Highway Traffic Safety Administration, April 1, 2024, https://www.nhtsa.gov/press-releases/2022-traffic-deaths-2023-early-estimates#:~:text=In%20 2022%2C%203%2C308%20people%20were,but%20it%20is%20also%20preventable.

If you're using your phone for GPS, set your location and activate it before you leave Park. Simply put: Don't text and drive. Don't check your social media. Don't check your notifications or read your email—even if you're at a red light.

Ask yourself, "Isn't texting behind the wheel kind of a pathetic way to die?" Sending or reading a text will cause you to take your eyes off the road for at least five seconds, and those five seconds could spell life or death. I promise you, the texts and social media posts will still be there after you get to your destination. Everyone thinks they're invincible until something terrible happens to them. iPhones can also send automated text messages indicating that you're driving and are unavailable for calls or texts if messages come in while you're on the road; enable this function under the Focus settings on your phone.

A Message from My Heart

When I was in high school, I experienced the devastating loss of one of my soccer coaches to a completely preventable tragedy. He was twenty seven years old, with his entire future ahead of him. However, he was texting and driving and also not wearing a seat belt. He lost control of his vehicle, veered off the road into a ditch, and was ejected through the windshield. This happened shortly before I was set to get my driver's permit, and it profoundly shaped my perspective on road safety. It was a heartbreaking reminder of how a single, avoidable decision can have irreversible consequences.

When You're Driving, *Drive*

DO NOT text and drive.

DO NOT do your makeup and drive.

DO NOT paint your nails and drive.

DO NOT eat and drive.

DO NOT turn around to tend to a crying child and drive. Yes, I am a mom and just said that. Better that your child is unhappy for a minute than unsafe.

If you must do anything other than drive, find a safe place to pull over!

Home Garage Safety

Whenever I pull into my garage, I wait in my car with the doors locked until the garage door is fully closed, and then I get out. This gives me an added layer of protection in case someone's lurking nearby, ready to slip into the garage. If someone does manage to get into the garage, I'm in my locked car, able to open the garage door and reverse myself out of the situation.

If your garage is attached to your home, this is one of the easiest ways someone can break into your house. If your car has a built-in garage door opener, avoid programming it, and never leave the actual garage door opener remote in your car. If your car is broken into or stolen, a thief could use the programmed system or the remote to access your garage and potentially enter your home. It's a small precaution that can prevent a bigger problem.

Instead of leaving your garage door opener inside your vehicle, buy a garage opener key chain. It's affordable and easy to use, and you can carry it around with you at all times, which is a far safer option.

Don't store your actual address in your GPS—instead, program the address to a nearby gas station, pharmacy, or other business near your home. Finally, always lock the door that leads from your garage to your house, and always keep your car locked, even if it's in your garage.

Real-World Safety Story

> Several months ago, I ran my car through the car wash. It was around 6:30 a.m. After driving through the wash, I pulled around to the area where they have towels and vacuums. I pulled up next to the one other car there, assuming it belonged to one of the car wash workers.
>
> I got out of my car and started to dry it off when I noticed a man in a hoodie get out of the other car. He moved around to the trunk area of his car as he stared at me intently. I immediately knew he was not right, so I got in my car from the passenger side, quickly closed the driver door from inside, and locked my doors. I drove away right then, calling my sister to tell her what happened.
>
> About a month later, I saw the same man on the news. He had been identified and subsequently arrested for stabbing a Phoenix police officer in the neck at a convenience store. This man had also tried to hijack a car in my neighborhood weeks before that.
>
> —Lisa

THE TAKEAWAY
Using your car as a barrier is a great line of defense.

Don't Pull Over for an Unmarked Car

For less than $30, anyone can buy fake police lights and sirens online. If you're ever being pulled over by an unmarked car and aren't sure if it's a real police officer, don't pull over right away. Instead, put on your hazard lights, move into the right lane, slow down slightly, and call 911 to confirm their identity. Do not stop until the 911 operator verifies that the person behind you is in fact a police officer. Taking this step ensures your safety in uncertain situations.

Getting gas safely

- Choose well-lit, busy gas stations whenever you can, and try to get gas only during the daytime.
- Keep your windows shut.
- After exiting your car, and before handling the gas pump, touch metal. This helps discharge any static electricity that could ignite a fire.
- This might be a me thing, but whenever I'm filling up my gas tank, I try not to stand next to my car. Instead, I get out, lock the car, start the pump, and then get back inside and lock the door while I wait. If getting back in the car isn't feasible for you, the most important thing is to stay alert and use this time to practice situational awareness—don't stand there zoning out and scrolling on your phone. Be fully present and aware of your surroundings.
- If a situation arises that makes you feel unsafe, use your horn to draw attention to yourself. Similarly, if this happens

when you're standing at the pump, you can use the gas itself as a weapon. This is a last resort, but spray away.

- If you find yourself in a truly dangerous situation and need to flee the scene while the gas is still pumping, you can drive off quickly and safely without worry; almost all gas pumps have breakaway valves in place that will instantly stop the flow of gasoline.

- Whenever possible, use Apple Pay or another touch-to-pay method at the gas pump for added security. If you need to use a physical credit card, take a moment to inspect the card reader before swiping or inserting your card. Check for anything unusual, like loose parts, scratches, or attachments that look out of place. These could be skimmer devices designed to steal your card information and PIN. A quick inspection can go a long way in protecting your finances.

- If you're charging an electric vehicle, choose a populated and well-lit station as you'll be sitting stationary for several minutes. Check for any loose wires or tampering. Always reverse-park if you're able, as this will allow you to better stay aware of your surroundings and exit quickly if needed. As usual, stay off your phone.

If someone attempts to carjack you . . .

If you're inside your car when someone tries to approach, don't hesitate—drive away immediately. However, if someone approaches you while you're outside your vehicle and demands access to your car, stay calm and comply with letting them take the car. Always assume an individual is armed, even if you don't see a weapon. Remember, your life is far more valuable than your car. However, if your kids are inside, it's time to fight, no holds barred.

I personally keep a tracking device like an Apple AirTag or a Tile tracker hidden inside my car so I can track its location in case of an emergency.

> ### Don't Fall for It
>
> If you ever come upon a stroller or a car seat on the side of the road, do not get out of your car. Instead, call 911—don't attempt to handle the situation yourself. Criminals are getting increasingly creative with their strategies to lure drivers out of their vehicles. Leaving a stroller or car seat on the side of the road could be a setup.

The Fender-Bender Con

If someone rear-ends you and you sense that something is off—or if it's simply late, dark, or there aren't many other drivers around—turn on your hazard lights and stay in the car with the doors locked. Call 911 right away, and, if possible, move to a main street before pulling over. If it's safe to do so, keep your car running so you can quickly leave if anything seems amiss. There have been documented cases of criminals intentionally causing minor accidents to lure victims out of their cars.

This is why I insist that you always trust your instincts in unpredictable situations like these. If this scenario happened to me, I'd have the other driver follow me to the nearest gas station, fire station, or other well-lit, well-populated area while I stayed on the phone with 911. I'd also keep my hazards on and my doors locked until I felt safe.

If you're being followed while driving . . .

- Stay on main roads that are well lit and well populated.

- Never go straight home (you don't want them knowing where you live, right?), and don't go to a friend or family member's house (same idea).

- Hop on the phone with 911 and head to the nearest fire station or police station.

- Keep your doors and windows locked, and no matter what you do, don't pull over or get out of the car.

- Maintain a calm demeanor and don't let the situation escalate (don't flip off the other driver, and don't curse or yell out your window).

Always Leave Yourself an "Out"

An "out" is simply an escape route, a way to remove yourself quickly from a potentially dangerous situation. This becomes especially important at stop signs and traffic lights. By leaving ample space between your vehicle and the one in front of you, you preserve your ability to act if something escalates. Situations on the road can shift in an instant, and that buffer may be the very thing that allows you to get out safely.

The Left-Turn Rule

This rule is something my grandma taught my dad, and my dad passed down to me. When you're stopped in traffic waiting to make a left turn, always keep your wheels pointed straight ahead; never angle them left in anticipation. If you're rear-ended while waiting and your wheels are already turned, your car will be pushed directly into oncoming traffic. Keeping them straight ensures you're pushed forward, not into danger.

Be Aware of Blind Spots

Driving around large vehicles like semitrucks can be nerve-racking, but if you're going to navigate safely around them, then it's crucial that you know where the blind spots are:

- The front blind spot is the area within about twenty feet in front of the truck's cab. If you can't see the headlights in your rearview mirror, the driver can't see you, so always drive far enough ahead to stay visible.

- To avoid the rear blind spot, keep at least a four-second distance behind the truck and make sure you can see both of its side mirrors. If you're within thirty feet, the driver won't be able to see you.

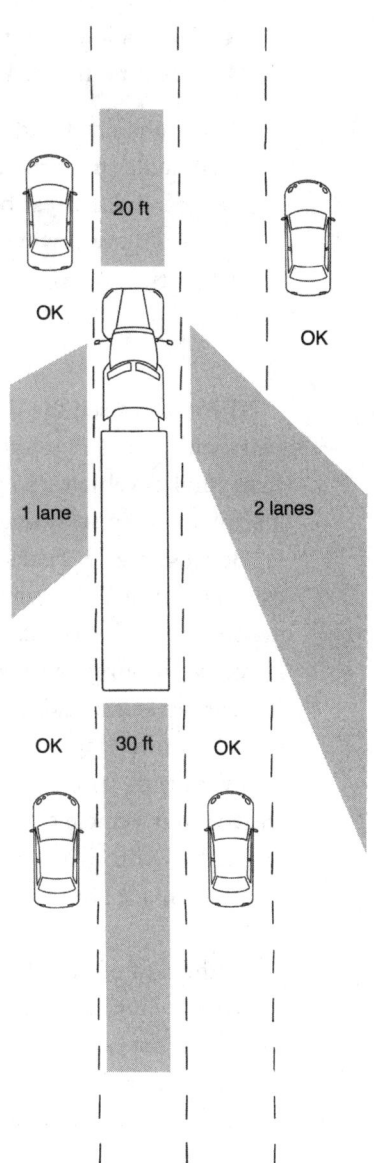

- The left-side blind spot extends from the middle of the trailer to about twenty feet behind the rear bumper in the lane next to the truck. It's best not to linger in this spot.
- The right-side blind spot is the largest and most dangerous. It stretches from the truck's passenger door to about twenty feet behind the rear bumper on the right side, and extends two lanes over. Avoid staying beside a truck on this side at all costs.

If you can't see the driver in their side mirrors, they can't see you. And always remember that semis take much longer to stop than smaller vehicles, so give them plenty of space. When passing a semi, do so quickly and decisively.

Because these trucks always demand space, you need to be especially mindful of giving them extra space when driving conditions are poor (for example, dark roads or hazardous weather). If you're in bumper-to-bumper traffic, no matter what types of vehicles are surrounding you, aim to stay in the outer right-hand lane. If you're stopped and there's a shoulder or grassy area beside you, turn your wheels to the right. That way, if you're rear-ended, your vehicle gets pushed out of the lane, not into the one in front of you. Most importantly, always leave at least a car's length of space ahead of you, even in gridlock. This space is your out.

At the end of the day, whether it's a semitruck, a small car, or a van, it's your responsibility to take care of your own safety—never assume someone else can see you. Every vehicle has its own individual blind spots, and your best bet is to always drive as defensively as possible.

The *Final Destination* Tip

If you're ever driving behind a truck carrying a large load, such as lumber, rolled steel, or other oversize or heavy objects, do not linger behind or next to them. Pass them soon as a safe opportunity presents itself. There have been instances where a truck's load has become dislodged, causing fatal accidents. In fact, this exact type of tragedy happened to the mother of my mom's friend. Think *Final Destination* . . . gulp! Avoid driving behind gravel trucks and other kinds of heavy equipment too—all you need is for a stone to be kicked up and hit your windshield.

PSAs for Parents

- Develop the habit of thoroughly checking around your vehicle each time you enter it to ensure that a child or pet has not unexpectedly moved into a potentially life-threatening scenario. (It's also a great way to keep from running over your kid's bike or toys.)

- Teach your kids not to assume that a school bus or any other vehicle will stop for them. From an early age, emphasize that they should never trust that any driver will stop for them; it's their responsibility to wait until there's no traffic before crossing the street. Encourage them to make direct eye contact with a driver before crossing the street at a stop sign or stoplight, including with the school bus driver right after they've gotten off the bus. Kids learn best from visual demonstrations, so try acting it out with your child in your own driveway. Just because a driver is supposed to stop doesn't mean they always will, and small children can be difficult to see, especially on the side of the road. Teach your kids to use the crosswalk whenever possible—and to cross with a group when they can—so they're easily visible.

- Tell your kids to stay off their phones and stay aware of their surroundings when they're walking to and from school or crossing any street. This type of situational awareness will stay with your children for the rest of their lives. When I was a kid, my parents and I played "I Spy" all the time, which helped me learn to notice vehicles, people, and other small details about the world around me.

- Always lock your car doors, even when your car is sitting in the driveway or garage. Kids love to play in cars and can get accidentally locked inside without your knowledge. This can quickly become a life-threatening situation, especially during the summer months.

- Never leave your kids or pets unattended in your car, even if you're just running inside to grab a coffee. In just thirty seconds, a vehicle can be stolen. Always take your children and pets with you, no matter what. Many places have strict laws against leaving pets unattended in cars. If you're going someplace where pets aren't allowed, the safest option is to leave your pet at home.

The Two-Second Rule

When a light turns green, wait a couple of seconds before moving to make sure that nobody is running through the opposing red light. This simple habit can save your life. Though this might annoy the driver behind you, I'd rather get honked at than smashed, wouldn't you?

Road Rage: It's All About Mindset

We've all felt or encountered road rage at some point. I've certainly felt my temper flare when another driver cut me off or did something frustrating—the urge to react is strong. But remember that nothing on the road is worth your life.

Before you get into your car, take a moment to breathe and shift your mindset. Decide that for the entire time you're behind the wheel, you're going to let things go. Whether you're driving for five minutes or five hours, remind yourself not to take anything personally. This small shift could literally save your life. While you can't control the actions of others, you do have control over your own behavior and attitude behind the wheel. A moment of anger is never worth risking a life-changing incident.

If you sense another driver is engaging in road rage toward you, don't respond in kind. Stay calm, keep driving, and avoid eye contact. Don't react to their provocations, no matter how tempting it may be. The other driver wants to provoke you—don't let them win. Keep your cool. Check your ego at the door.

Road Rage on the Rise

Between 2014 and 2023, the rate of road-rage-related shootings skyrocketed by more than 400 percent.[*]

When Trouble Strikes

Prepare, prepare, prepare. While you can't control everything that happens on the road, you can—and should—take whatever precautions you can to ensure you're as safe as possible when behind the wheel of your car. Replace that worn windshield wiper *before* you're caught in a downpour in rush-hour traffic. But sometimes, no matter how well we've prepared, things happen. Below are tips on preparing for the worst and advice on what to do when trouble strikes.

On a road trip

- Ensure your vehicle is well maintained before hitting the road. Check your oil, tire pressure, wipers, and your windshield fluid. Consider taking your car in for a quick inspection before you hit the road.

- Keep a trusted friend, family member, or partner informed about your whereabouts at all times. Sharing your location makes this easy.

---

[*] Jennifer Mascia and Chip Brownlee, "Road Rage Shootings Have Surged over the Past Decade," Trace, April 25, 2024, https://www.thetrace.org/2024/04/road-rage-shooting-gun-highway-deaths/.

- For rest areas and gas stations, choose locations that are well lit and populated. Try to do your research about rest areas beforehand; some states have gas stations at rest areas and some don't.

- Refuel well before you need it.

- If you need to stop overnight, book your accommodations in advance.

- Always lock your doors—car doors, hotel doors, all of them!

- Travel with whatever form of personal protection you feel comfortable carrying (see page 207).

If your car breaks down . . .

Your safety is always the priority. If you have car trouble, pull over to the side of the road as far away from traffic as possible and stay in your vehicle with your seat belt on and your hazard lights flashing to alert other drivers. Call for help immediately—whether it's 911, roadside assistance, or a tow truck. If your car starts smoking or catches fire, get everyone out as quickly as possible. Don't wait! Check for traffic, exit on the passenger side if you can, and move to a safe distance of at least one hundred feet.

If a power line falls on your car . . .

Always assume a power line is live. Your first instinct will be to exit your vehicle, but in this case, it's safest to stay put to avoid getting electrocuted. Call 911.

DOWNED POWERLINE ON YOUR CAR?

NO SMOKE OR FIRE

Stay put inside your vehicle. Do not touch anything and call 911 immediately.

SMOKE OR FIRE

STEP 1: *Unbuckle and open your door without touching metal. Get into a crouched jump position with your feet together.*

BUCKLE UP 49

 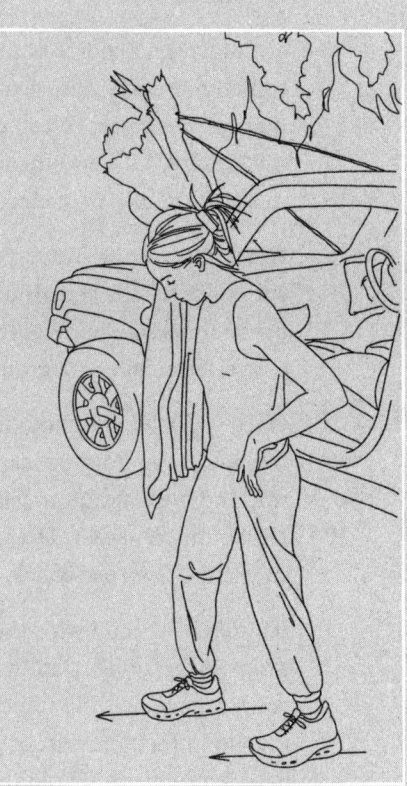

STEP 2: *Leap away from your vehicle. Do NOT touch the car and the ground simultaneously (land with BOTH feet together).*

STEP 3: *Keep your feet planted and shuffle away from your vehicle. Do not lift your feet. Move a safe distance away.*

- Remain in your car and call 911; then wait for help.

- Keep your hands and feet inside your vehicle. Avoid contact with any metal parts of the car.

- *Never* touch any part of the power line or the equipment connected to it.

- If you have no choice but to exit the vehicle due to smoke or fire, unbuckle your seat belt and open the door, but make sure no part of you or your clothes or gear touches the ground. This and the following steps are meant to minimize your risk of electric shock.

- Next, jump as far away from the vehicle as you can, landing with both feet on the ground at the same time (make sure not to touch the body of the car). Your primary goal here is to avoid touching the ground and the car simultaneously.

- Once you land with both feet on the ground, shuffle at least fifty feet away from the car. Make sure your feet are side by side and both always touching the ground as you shuffle. Do not lift your feet. Doing all the above helps minimize your risk of electric shock.

- If you have a child with you and they're old enough to copy what you're doing, lead by example and have them follow your steps to exit the vehicle safely. If they're too small for that, hold them in your arms while you exit the car. If you have pets with you, hold them (if they're small enough) or gently toss them away from the vehicle.

Don't Exit Your Vehicle

One of my dad's best high school friends was in the US Army. His friend was with another soldier when their vehicle broke down, and he did what so many of us might do in that situation: He got out to push the car from behind while his buddy steered. But in a heartbreaking moment, a distracted driver didn't see them and crashed into them from behind, killing my dad's friend instantly. This devastating loss is a reminder I'll never forget: Unless it's a life-or-death emergency, don't get out of your car on a busy road. No matter how capable or careful you think you are, the risks are just too great; you can't control what other people do. Stay in your vehicle and call for help. Nothing is worth more than your life.

If you get stranded in your car...

- Stay put in the car if it's safe to do so. Keep the doors locked and call for help if you have service.

- If you don't have cell service, try using satellite calling or texting if your phone supports it. This allows you to communicate even when you don't have cell service or Wi-Fi, typically in remote areas with no cell towers, by connecting directly to a satellite. You need to have a clear view of the sky to use this function.

- Remember: Leave the car to look for help only as a last resort. It's safer to stay put and wait for help. Use flares (they should be in your roadside emergency kit—see below) to let others know you're stuck and in need of assistance.

Emergency items to always keep in your car

- An emergency first-aid kit
- Your car's user manual
- Your license (keep it with you), registration, and proof of insurance
- A blanket (if you have other people in your car with you, use one another for body heat)
- Water and snacks
- An empty container that can be used to urinate in, in case you can't exit your vehicle
- A roadside emergency kit—know what's in it and how to use those items (if you ever need it, you'll be happy you thought ahead)
- A functioning flashlight
- A portable charger that doesn't use the car as a source of power
- An emergency hand-crank radio to stay aware of weather issues in case you lose service or your car battery dies
- Personal protection: pepper gel or your item of choice (see page 209; always remember to abide by your local laws regarding personal protection)
- A car escape tool (window breaker/seat belt cutter)
- A spare tire and a jack (if you don't have run-flat tires)
- An ice scraper and small shovel (if you live in a part of the country that gets snow in the winter)

Keeping Cars Locked While in Park

Make it a habit to lock your car doors as soon as you get in, and then keep them locked while you're inside, no matter where you are. It's a simple precaution that can enhance your safety and give you peace of mind.

Some cars feature doors that automatically unlock when the car is put in park. This can pose a safety hazard; remember, *your car doors should always be locked* when you're inside. If your vehicle automatically unlocks when you park it, read your user manual to see if there's a way to disable this feature. If not, consult with your local dealership or auto repair shop to see if they can disable it for you.

Going Incognito

You don't want to give strangers any information about your family, and this definitely goes for signage on cars. While "stick family" decals on your back windshield might not seem like a big deal, you never know who you might cross paths with. It's my belief that the less personal information you publicly display, the better. The same goes for college, sorority, or school sports decals. It's in your best interest to keep your car as simple and unadorned as possible. Your vehicle shouldn't say anything about you personally.

Don't leave anything with your name or address on it visibly lying around your car. This includes mail, prescriptions, tickets, IDs, or work badges. Leaving these and other sorts of "harmless" items lying around can also be a magnet for theft. Even small objects like car chargers, spare change, hoodies, or makeup bags could be enticing for a thief because they indicate that you might have other more valuable goodies stashed away. Reduce your risk of having your identity compromised and lower the chance of a car break-in by keeping your vehicle as uncluttered and identity-free as possible.

> **Feet on the Floor!**
>
> *Never* put your feet up on the dash when you're riding in the passenger's seat. If the car gets in an accident, causing the airbags to deploy, sitting this way could cause catastrophic damage to your legs, hips, and other parts of your body. Sitting up properly with your seat belt on can mean the difference between walking away from an accident or not.

Parking Lot Safety

Parking lots are transitional spaces, and they can easily attract predators. If someone tries to abduct you, a "thinking outside the box" defensive technique is to grab ahold of a grocery cart (or any other large object) and latch on—it's nearly impossible for someone to take both you and the cart, and you'll make lots of clatter-y noise.

When you're in a parking lot . . .

- Park in well-lit, well-populated areas and always be aware of your surroundings.
- If there is one, park near the cart return rack to create a physical barrier.
- Lock your car doors immediately when getting in and out of your vehicle.
- When returning to your vehicle, watch for cars parked on your driver's side that are too close for comfort. This puts you in a vulnerable position should someone try to grab you.
- Keep an eye out for people loitering or watching you a little too closely.
- Don't linger in your car or get distracted by your phone. Stay alert and focused.
- Keep your personal protection easily accessible.
- Always have your keys ready when you are returning to your car.
- If you feel unsafe, head back into the store. Never be afraid to ask for help.
- Take a photo of your parking spot and the level of the lot or garage you're in, so you'll be able to find your car more easily when you come back.

The Triangle Method of Grocery Shopping

The triangle method is a tactic for loading groceries into your car that entails putting up a protective barrier in the form of a triangle between you and those around you. The triangle consists of the inside of your open door, the cart positioned between

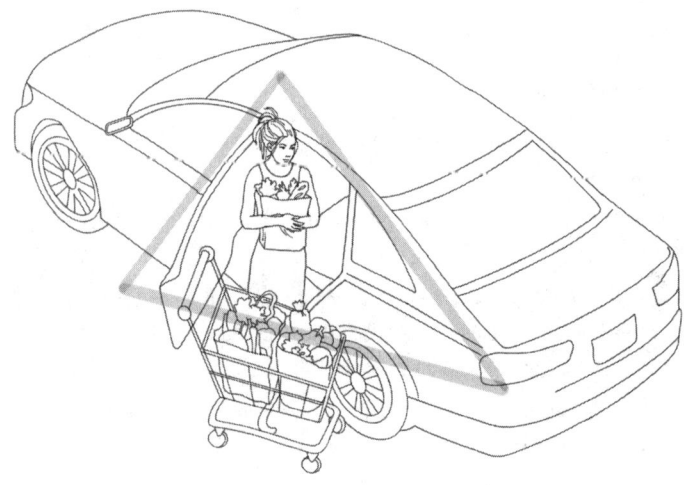

your car and the door, and the open area of your vehicle into which you are placing the groceries; position yourself on the inside of the triangle formed by your car, your door, and the cart. Keep all the other doors locked. This allows you to stay aware of your surroundings. Remember, if need be, the cart can be used not only as a barrier but also as a weapon: By thrusting or kicking the cart, you can create the distance and time needed to hop into your vehicle, lock the door behind you, climb into the driver's seat, and get out of there.

Real-World Safety Story

Earlier this year I was in Washington, DC, at a conference. After an intense day of learning, I was exhausted. When I got to the underground parking garage, I realized I had misplaced my car.

I started walking in circles, panicking as I struggled to remember where I parked.

To make matters worse, I was in the wrong garage—one block off—but it was owned by the same company, so it looked identical. As I wandered, I noticed a man lingering near a stairwell. He wasn't heading to a car or the exit—just watching.

The longer I stayed lost, the more disoriented I became, and the more aware I was that he was still there. My gut screamed that something wasn't right.

Instead of continuing to wander, I stopped, pulled out my phone, called a friend, and loudly stated where I was. I walked briskly toward the garage entrance, making sure to stay in view of the security cameras. As soon as I got back to street level, I asked a building security guard for help. The man quickly disappeared.

—Kimberly

THE TAKEAWAY

Take a photo or make a note of where you park. Also, if you feel unsafe, try to stay in view of cameras, and never be afraid to ask security for help. Remember, in a dangerous situation, noise is your friend.

Swipe Smart

The New Rules of Dating Safely

Online dating is more popular than ever—almost 50 percent of Americans have tried it, and statistically speaking, it's how most couples meet these days. I met my husband on social media; little did we know, we lived two blocks from each other, went to the same gym, and had probably crossed paths a hundred times. But eventually it was social media that brought us together. I can personally vouch for the internet being a solid way of making connections.

But with that said, meeting people online does introduce a new and different set of risks. This chapter will help you safely navigate the world of dating, both on and offline.

First-Date Safety

First dates can run the gamut from fun to awkward to nerve-racking to awful. Before you meet up with anyone, you'll want to take these precautions:

> **DO SOME DIGGING.** Before you go on a date with someone, find out their full name and look them up! Back in the day, my friends and family knew me as the Dating FBI; they'd always joke that if someone gave me a first name, I could have details, down to that person's blood type, back to them by noon. Remember, Google is your friend; don't be shy about doing a little reconnaissance (you don't have to tell the person what you've uncovered). Look up their social media profiles on every platform, including LinkedIn, and make sure they are who they say they are. You don't have to find out the house they grew up in or their mother's maiden name. You just want to make sure they're not lying, catfishing, using a fake identity, or—worst-case scenario—a felon. If you want to do a deeper dive into someone's background and are willing to pay a fee, there are many web services that provide this.

> **IF YOU ACCEPTED A DATE BUT HAVE CHANGED YOUR MIND ABOUT IT, LIE TO SURVIVE!** Come up with a polite excuse for why you can't make it. Feel empowered to change your mind at any time; consent doesn't apply only to sexual situations. You can also revoke consent to go out with someone before or even during a date.

> **MAKE SURE YOU TELL A TRUSTED PERSON THAT YOU'RE GOING ON A DATE.** They should know where and when you're going, and with whom. Have a friend or relative on standby whom you can ask to call you if you text them saying you need an "out." This person should also be waiting at the end of the night to hear you've made it home safely. If they don't hear from you, they'll know there's an issue and that they should act. For extra safety, you have the option of sharing your location with your trusted person.

- **DON'T LET YOUR DATE PICK YOU UP OR DRIVE YOU HOME.** You don't want them to know where you live, you don't want to be dependent on them to get home, and it's never the best idea to be confined in a small, locked space with a stranger.

- **BRING PERSONAL PROTECTION LIKE PEPPER GEL OR PEPPER SPRAY WITH YOU.** You probably won't need it, but it's better to be safe than sorry!

- **DON'T MEET YOUR DATE AT THEIR PLACE.** No need to be stuck in a stranger's home in a random, unfamiliar neighborhood. Tell your date you're coming from elsewhere and would prefer to meet them at the location you've selected.

- **DON'T SHARE AN UBER WITH YOUR DATE** or let your date call you an Uber. Again, you never want to disclose your home address.

- **MEET SOMEWHERE WELL POPULATED, LIKE A POPULAR BAR, CAFE, OR RESTAURANT.** Consider having coffee or drinks instead of dinner. Dinner can drag out for hours; on a first date, brevity is best. Don't go somewhere you could potentially be isolated, and don't even think about going on a hike or a drive! If you want to be outside on your date, try walking around a tourist neighborhood in your town or city or checking out a fair or a performance in a park. Just be sure there are lots of people around.

- **HAVE A DRINK IF YOU WANT ONE, BUT DON'T GET DRUNK.** It's best to have your head on straight when meeting new people. (Also, beer goggles are a thing!)

- **ALWAYS WATCH YOUR DRINK.** Consume only a beverage that you watched the bartender make. In other words, don't let your date handle your drink without your eyes remaining on it at all times. Don't ever leave your drink unattended, even if you're getting up to go to the restroom. (I discuss this in more detail on page 73.)

- **DON'T GIVE OUT YOUR REAL PHONE NUMBER RIGHT AWAY.** Your cell phone number is publicly linked to all sorts of personal information about you, including your full name and home address, so don't give out your number until you truly trust someone. Either keep messaging someone using the app (if you met through one), or get an anonymous number through Google Voice or a similar app.

- **DON'T OVERSHARE ON A FIRST DATE.** This person doesn't need to know what exact building you live in, the make and model of your car, the gym you belong to—you get the gist. It's safer to reveal only the rudimentary basics on a first date. Ask them more questions and get to know them first. If there's a question you're uncomfortable with, try pivoting the question back to them. For example, if they ask what gym you go to, you could reply, "I'm looking to join a gym—do you have any recommendations?"

- **DON'T GO HOME WITH SOMEONE AT THE END OF A FIRST DATE.** I'm not being prudish, but you *are* taking a safety risk if you go home with someone you don't know. Again, no judgment—this is purely a safety issue.

Using Pepper Gel or Spray

If you're going to carry pepper gel or spray, knowing in advance how to use it is crucial, and be sure to check if your state (and any state you want to enter while carrying it) has any restrictions on its use. I personally prefer pepper gel because there's less risk of blowback. Always use your thumb and not your pointer finger when deploying pepper gel or spray. In a high-stress situation, your pointer finger will be far less accurate, making it much easier to spray yourself in the face. Never do a test spray under duress—you don't want to walk through the cloud or accidentally spray yourself. Use it only when you're ready to go. Remember to always keep your gel or spray nearby and easily accessible. (See more on this and other forms of self-defense in A List of Safety Tools on page 207.)

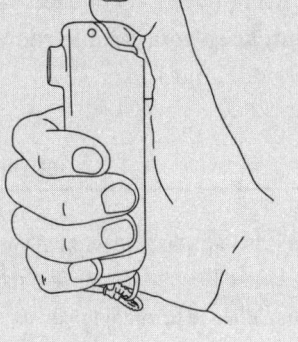

Always use your thumb when deploying pepper gel or spray.

Online and App Dating

Meeting a literal stranger for one-on-one drinks or dinner would have been unthinkable fifty years ago, outside of a blind date set up by friends, but these days almost every single person who's looking for love does this regularly. Keep these tips in mind when you're entering the wild world of online and app dating.

The less information you reveal on your profile, the better. There's absolutely no reason for you to use your full name or to list your place of work, your university, or the neighborhood where you live.

Instead of your full name, try using a nickname that is a play off your real name (like "Dani" instead of "Dannah"). Make sure your car, home, apartment complex, and other identifiable features aren't visible in the background of your photos, and don't post pictures of yourself hanging out in traceable spots near your home, like local parks, shops, or restaurants.

If you include a photo of your pet, make sure its tags don't divulge your name, address, and phone number.

Be mindful of the pics you're posting. I suggest refraining from using overly sexualized photos that can be misinterpreted; instead, keep your profile more PG-rated. Maintain the vibe of professional but fun.

Seriously, Don't Overshare

> The less info you reveal about yourself on your online dating profile, the better. Keep it vague. This makes you more mysterious and alluring while also keeping you safer.

Reading Between the Lines of Someone's Profile

Men taking mirror selfies or holding up their catch of the day are online-dating stereotypes for a reason: because they happen all the time. While clichés like these aren't necessarily signs of danger, they could be signs of arrogance or even narcissistic traits. If someone looks, acts, or speaks like a jerk on their profile, they're probably a jerk. Pay attention to the following tip-offs when you're checking out someone's profile:

- **WATCH OUT FOR PHOTOS THAT ARE GRAINY OR UNDECIPHERABLE.** What's this person hiding? Also, be wary of someone who looks different in each of their photos. They may be trying to disguise themselves or pretend they're someone else. If their profile contains little to no written information, consider it a flag—they might not be who they say they are, or they could be a catfish.

- **IF YOU'RE A HETEROSEXUAL WOMAN, WATCH THE WAY A MAN TALKS ABOUT WOMEN, BOTH ON THEIR PROFILE AND IN PERSON.** If someone bashes their exes, their mom, or other women on dating apps; generalizes about women as a subpopulation; or shows any sign of having resentment issues, steer clear. Remember, he's the common denominator! If he's always in the right and they're always in the wrong, it's most likely his issue, not theirs.

- **LOOK OUT FOR STRAY WEDDING RINGS!** Sometimes people forget to crop them out in photos.

- **IF SOMEONE MENTIONS MONEY OR FINANCES ON THEIR PROFILE— EITHER THEIRS OR YOURS—BE WARY.** They could be looking for a meal ticket . . . or assuming that you are.

- **WATCH HOW THEY SPEAK ABOUT THEMSELVES.** If they don't write much about themselves, instead focusing entirely on what they expect from a date or what their future partner should bring to the table, it's a potential sign of selfishness. Why do you have to prove yourself before they've given you a reason to trust them?

Red Flags to Look Out for on a Date

If a date is bragging a lot, being too cocky or arrogant, or laying it on too thick, or if it all seems too good to be true, it probably is. Here are some warning signs:

- Love-bombing. Your date tells you during your first get-together that they want to meet your parents one day? This person doesn't even know *you*; how could they possibly know that they want to meet your parents? Love-bombing is showering you with too much too soon. And it's a red flag.

- Attempts to isolate. If there's any talk of trying to get you to go somewhere private soon after you've met someone, it's a bad sign. You don't know this person well enough to trust. Don't go!

- Sexual references. Is your date making sexual references too quickly? Are they aware of your discomfort? Be clear on both your intentions and theirs.

Script It Out

> We've all been there. You're an hour in with a date and it dawns on you that not only are you not enjoying this person's company, but something about them is creeping you out. It's okay if you can't put your finger on it; that's your intuition kicking in, and you're allowed to cut things short.

You don't want to show your hand or let the person know you're bothered, so practice what I preach: Lie to survive, as described in chapter 2. Come up with an excuse and get out of there. Here's a scripted example:

You: "Hey, I'm having a really nice time, but I'm getting a horrible migraine, so I'll need to head home in a sec."

Your date: "Oh, I hope it's nothing serious..."

You: "I get them all the time and they're pretty awful. I don't want to keep you if I'm not at my best. I'm sorry to cut this short."

Your date: "Oh, I see. Well, I'll drive you home."

You: "Thanks for offering, but I texted my brother and he's on his way."

Don't leave alone, however—ask a friend to pick you up or quietly call an Uber from the bathroom. Never let your date drive or walk you home.

Stalking

There are distinct types of stalkers, and not all of them are the kinds we typically hear about in news stories. A stalker who targets celebrities is quite different from an acquaintance or romantic stalker who actually knows you. An *acquaintance stalker* has seen you out and about and for whatever reason is drawn to you. This is someone you know—maybe someone you worked with, went to school with, or have simply seen around town or met through someone else. A *romantic stalker* could be a former partner, a date, or someone you romantically rejected in some way.

If you feel you're being stalked by a date, a former or current romantic partner, or anyone else . . .

- Always stay aware of your surroundings when you're out. Keep your head up and stay conscious of what's going on around you (and behind you!).

- Never ignore a stalker or assume they'll go away on their own. They might not, and your safety is top priority.

- Don't engage with the person at all. Don't respond to their texts or phone calls, and don't acknowledge them online. Block their phone number and block them on social media as well.

- Don't post in real time on social media. Make sure your account is private and not easily found. Try changing your handle and your photo so it's not clear that your account belongs to you. Reduce your posting frequency and *never* tag your location.

- Don't keep the stalking a secret. Tell your family and friends what's going on and make sure they know not to interact with the stalker. It's vital that everyone close to you keep your personal information private and not accidentally leak where you live, where you work, where you work out, and so on. Make sure everyone who's close to you is aware of what's happening and continue to keep them in the loop.

- Save every communication you receive from the stalker—any notes, texts, emails, voicemails, or other methods.

- Make your day-to-day life highly unpredictable. Don't go out at the same time every day. Don't take the same route to work, school, the gym, or other places you visit regularly. And try not to go places alone.

- Make sure you have a good home security system with a functional camera.
- Your doors and windows should always be locked, both at home and in your car.
- Don't try to handle a stalker by yourself; remember that early intervention is key. Seek help the moment you feel unsafe—and contact police if you're in immediate danger.

Real-World Safety Story

The year was 1976 and I was about sixteen years old. I had been invited to a concert by a boy I had been casually dating. He seemed like a nice guy, but I really wasn't that interested. He picked me up, but as we were driving, I noticed he wasn't driving to the venue. When I asked him where we were going, he said to pick up some of his friends. I replied, "So you guys will probably all be getting high and drinking while I'm the only girl in a car crammed with guys?" And he said "Yep." I firmly told him to turn around and take me home; he said no, that we'd have a great time. I was so angry, but I also felt terrified. I screamed at him to pull the car over and he did. I opened the door and ran.

—Anonymous

THE TAKEAWAY
Your safety is more important than anyone else's feelings.

Squad Safety

Going Out While Staying Safe

Most of us have had our share of wild nights (in my twenties, I most certainly did!), but it's crucial to balance fun with safety. This chapter will explain how you can party with friends responsibly and safely. I'll share the essential dos and don'ts I've learned from my own experiences as a young woman as well as from my own research and education. It's not just about having a good time—paying attention while drinking or partying is key to ensuring that your nights out are both fun and secure.

By following these tips, you can let the good times roll while also minimizing your risks:

- **HAVE A CHECK-IN PERSON.** Before you go out, appoint a reliable check-in person you can text or call at the end of the night. Someone always needs to hear from you when you get home. This person should be a parent, brother, sister, or friend who is *not* part of your group that evening. Decide on this person ahead of time and promise to let them know when you're home safely, no matter how late it is or how tired you might be.

- **LEAVE FLASHY ACCESSORIES AT HOME.** Wearing your most expensive jewelry or carrying your fanciest handbag on a night out with the girls is a no-no. You might not be in the right mindset to keep close tabs on them, and you're calling attention to yourself in an unsafe way—potentially making yourself a target for theft. There's a time and a place for everything, but barhopping is not the occasion to show off your most luxe possessions. Opting for more discreet, practical options not only reduces your risk of loss or theft but also allows you to focus on having fun.

- **THIS IS ANOTHER TIME TO BRING YOUR PERSONAL SECURITY DEVICES WITH YOU.** I suggest bringing pepper gel and a personal key chain alarm. Keep them in a place that's easy to reach, and if you ever feel like you're in immediate danger, don't be afraid to use them.

- **SITUATIONAL AWARENESS IS YOUR FIRST LINE OF DEFENSE.** Anytime you arrive in a new place, whether it's a bar, restaurant, airport, concert venue, or anywhere else, take ten seconds to mentally familiarize yourself with your immediate surroundings. Take note of all the exits, then scan the space and look at everyone around you. Does anyone give you a weird vibe? Is there anything that feels off? If something or someone truly makes you uncomfortable, make a mental note and trust your gut. Consider leaving if you're getting an overwhelmingly negative vibe. If you see or sense something off, say something.

- **WATCH YOUR DRINK.** As mentioned on page 62, whenever you're out in public, watch your drink like a hawk. (You can also invest in a special tool that looks like a scrunchie but doubles as an anti-spiking drink cover; see page 209.) If your drink leaves your line of vision, get a new one. You don't want to be drugged.

- **HAVE A DESIGNATED SOBER FRIEND.** If you're going out in a group, take turns appointing a friend to be the group's designated sober leader for the night. This gives me a flashback to high school, when my friends were starting to experiment with alcohol (yes, I realize they were underage, and while I don't condone it, high school drinking happens). I was always the designated driver, not only because I didn't trust other people behind the wheel but because my main focus was soccer, so I walked a straight line. That said, I was still around drinking and partying all the time. As I got older and hit legal age, I realized more and more that a sober friend doesn't need to be entirely abstinent; they can have a social drink. Their job is to stay moderate and mindful of their drinking so they can be clear-headed enough to help scout for potential dangers (whether it's an ill-meaning stranger or something as simple as an uneven curb on the way out of the bar). They can help discourage other friends in the group from overindulging or wandering off, and they can make sound decisions if an emergency arises. They can arrange the group's transportation, whether that's driving, public transport, or a car service. They can also help if one person ends up drinking too much, and they can effectively speak to emergency services if a safety or medical issue pops up. As your sober buddy, they're the best-equipped person to make informed decisions and handle tough situations calmly.

That said, choose your crew wisely. When it comes to the "messy friend," I can speak from experience as I've dealt with several—from carrying out an unconscious body (yes, she was breathing) to being escorted from a club with a friend's head in a trash bag (due to excessive projectile vomiting). From stories I've heard, it seems the "messy friend" is somewhat universal.

If you have a female friend in this category (someone who overimbibes, gets super loud, or takes unnecessary risks), remember, you don't have to go out with her! But if you're already out with her, and especially if you're the designated driver, make it your top priority to get her home safely—someone in that "messy" state is unable to make safe, rational decisions. Safety is top priority. While no one wants to babysit a friend when you're going out to have a good time, when there's alcohol involved, bad decisions are sometimes inevitable. The goal is to always get everyone home safely at the end of the night.

Script It Out

HELPING THE "MESSY" FRIEND

If you have a friend for whom "messiness" becomes a pattern, talk to her if you're concerned about her alcohol intake or her behaviors when drinking—and bring up your worries at the right place and time. Her problematic behavior could put both you and her in a dangerous situation, and it could also be masking a deeper issue—it's possible your friend needs extra support (or just a good shoulder to cry on). Try to assess whether your friend's behavior is a cry for help. If so, assist her in getting the help she needs—never ignore or abandon a friend who's having a hard time.

If you're trying to have a tough conversation with a messy friend, you never want to say anything accusatory. You'll want to approach it nonjudgmentally with empathy and consideration. You might say, "I've noticed lately when we go out, you drink more than you plan to. I've seen it really affect you emotionally the next day. I'm just wondering if you're okay or if you need someone to talk to. I'm here and I love you." If it seems like your friend isn't going to receive this feedback well, try this: "I'm not judging at all; I know life is stressful for us both right now. But I've noticed you seem to be drinking more than you usually do. Would you be open to doing more things together that don't involve going out? I love spending time with you and it doesn't always have to be at a bar. Why don't we grab sushi and have a beach picnic or something?" This is an invitation to allow your friend to be vulnerable and open up if they need to talk. If you love your friend but aren't close enough to address the issue directly, you could always tell her you're doing a sober reset and ask if she's open to hanging out in settings that don't involve alcohol.

- **NEVER LEAVE AN ESTABLISHMENT ALONE.** Preplan your end-of-night transportation before you go out, and be sure that when you leave, everyone is accounted for. Never walk home alone, especially at night. Establishing a clear plan for getting home in advance ensures that nobody is left in a vulnerable position. Also, be sure to communicate any change in plans with your group to make sure everyone stays safe. There's safety in numbers.

Social Media Safety

When you're going out with your girls, avoid posting on social media in real time—and never include your specific location in social media stories. Tagging your location or sharing updates as they happen makes it easy for strangers to track your whereabouts, which can put you at risk. And be sure to limit the amount of personal information you share online, such as details about the venue or the timing of your arrival or departure. Keep your plans private. We'll touch on this more on page 110.

- **USE GIRL CODES AND SECRET GESTURES.** An emergency code word can come in handy during a night out with your girls. It's a secret way to communicate to a friend that you're not feeling safe or comfortable. Choose a word that's easy to slip into common conversation but not so routine that you say it all the time (when I would go out with my friends, we always used something as simple as "banana" as our code word). You can also choose a gesture in addition to a word—having a secret gesture makes it easy to let your friends know you're uncomfortable, even from across a crowded room.

- **STICK TOGETHER, ESPECIALLY WHEN ALCOHOL IS INVOLVED.** You're less of a target when you're in a group, so make sure you stay together! Don't let your friends wander off or get separated. In the unpredictable environment of a night out, having a solid unit means that you can look out for one another, avoid potential dangers, and provide support if anyone runs into trouble. It's much easier to maintain situational awareness—

and make better decisions—when you have friends by your side. Go out together, hang out together, and leave together. On a similar note, make sure you have a bathroom buddy when you head to a restroom. Bringing a girlfriend (or three) can help stave off any unwanted scenarios.

> **KEEP YOUR STUFF SAFELY STASHED.** Don't hang your handbag on the back of a bathroom door—someone could reach over and grab it. Similarly, be cautious when hanging your bag from a bar hook; a determined thief could quickly swipe it if you're not vigilant. Essentially, always keep your stuff close to you—or physically on you!

If you need to put your bag down somewhere, keep it within reach. Avoid leaving important items like your credit cards, ID, or phone in plain view because this can attract unwanted attention and make it easier for someone to steal them. This advice might sound obvious, but you'd be surprised at how many times I've seen unattended bags left out in public.

> **HOW TO TELL IF YOU—OR SOMEONE AROUND YOU—HAS BEEN DRUGGED.** If you're out at a bar or party and notice a friend acting strange, there's a chance they've been drugged. Things to watch for include:

- Sudden changes in the person's behavior or mood, like extreme drowsiness, fatigue, agitation, confusion, or erratic actions.

- Physical signs, like slurred speech, difficulty walking, or impaired motor coordination, as well as vomiting, nausea, or dizziness.

- Lags in memory.

- Hallucinations or other seriously impaired sensory perceptions.

- "Drunken" behavior beyond what might be expected by the number of drinks consumed.

- If there are any obvious signs that a drink has been spiked, call 911—and don't throw the drink away. It could help law enforcement identify what substance was in it.

❱ **BAD GUYS DON'T ALWAYS LOOK LIKE BAD GUYS.** Keep your guard up—and watch out for people who seem unusually nice. Not trusting someone who's kind to you might sound counterintuitive, but if you or a friend is impaired and you notice someone going out of their way to rush over to "help" you, be wary. What's their motive? Even if they seem nice and helpful, they are still strangers, and nice doesn't necessarily mean safe. Be discerning about whom you'll accept help from.

Let's say you're out at a bar and you meet a guy who seems like the sweetest guy on earth. He's complimenting you like crazy and talking your ear off about how much he wants to get to know you or at least take you out for a nice dinner. This is all fine and dandy, but remember . . .

- If you just met him, you don't know him. Charm and charisma can sometimes be a cover for less savory psychological qualities, and serial killers like Ted Bundy lured their victims by being charming, handsome, and charismatic.

- Keep your wits about you. Don't isolate yourself with anyone you've just met.

- Make people earn your trust.

- Be discerning about whom you give your number to.
- Be even more discerning if you choose to leave with someone. Leaving with a stranger (whether you're going somewhere else with him or he's driving you home) opens you up to avoidable risks.

) **TRUST YOUR INSTINCTS WHEN YOU'RE OUT AND ABOUT.** If something feels off about a person or place, trust your gut—whether the dude you just met seems ever-so-slightly odd or the general vibe of the bar you're at is giving you the ick, follow your intuition. Your instincts are powerful indicators of potential danger and ignoring them can put you at risk. If you sense something isn't right, don't hesitate to take action, whether it's going someplace else, telling your friends you're uncomfortable, or even heading home. Prioritizing your safety by listening to your instincts helps you protect yourself and lets you maintain a sense of control over your surroundings.

) **MAKE A CHANGE OF VENUE.** If you or your friends feel unsafe at a certain location—or can't seem to shake a creeper—don't hesitate to leave. Your safety always comes first! If the atmosphere or a particular person feels off, trust your instincts and "exit stage left." There's absolutely no reason to stay somewhere you feel uncomfortable or threatened. Finding a safer, more welcoming environment not only helps you avoid potential risks but also ensures that you and your friends can continue having fun. Be proactive about changing up your location if something doesn't feel right.

) **STAY IN WELL-LIT LOCATIONS WHEN YOU'RE MOVING FROM PLACE TO PLACE.** You're more vulnerable in transitional spaces. If you need to step outside to make a phone call, stay in front of the restaurant; don't go around the corner or into an alley. If you and your friends are walking to another bar, stay on a sidewalk, preferably with streetlights and people. Make sure your rideshare is picking you up on a main street and not on a dark side road. It's not rocket science: Staying in well-lit areas reduces your chances of being a target of crime. Lighting enhances visibility, therefore making it harder for potential threats or criminal acts to go unnoticed. Good lighting also helps you spot potential dangers and recognize unfamiliar faces, and it allows you to be more alert to any unusual things happening around you.

Real-World Safety Story

One night a few years ago, my friend and I went barhopping with a group of people we met out. I consider myself pretty cautious, and by the end of the night we felt like these people were safe to be around.

We got into what they told us was an Uber, but instead of going to another bar, the car kept driving. I realized quickly this wasn't an Uber. That's when they said we were actually heading to an afterparty.

The house we arrived at was in a secluded, gated community, completely empty—no furniture, no doorknobs, nothing. And inside, there were about ten men. That's when I noticed my friend starting to lose her ability to speak. She just kept shaking her head, unable to form words. I knew we were in trouble. I had to think fast, so I pretended to be drunk so they wouldn't get suspicious.

I took my friend to the bathroom, but they kept trying to open the door. I faked a phone call, acting like I was bringing more girls to the party, which made them let their guard down. When they followed us outside, I told them I needed to grab a friend, who had been "dropped off at the wrong house." As soon as they went inside, I pulled my friend along and we sprinted. We turned a corner, hoping to find help, but all we found were bushes. That's when we heard them come back outside, yelling for us. We had no service, no way to call for help, so we hid in the bushes—rosebushes, of all things. We stayed there, completely still for three hours, until they finally gave up searching for us.

—Michaela

THE TAKEAWAY

Even if you initially feel safe in a situation or around a group of individuals you just met, be mindful of your alcohol or substance consumption. You need to retain the ability to detect if something is off.

Stay safe when hailing a rideshare or taxi

- When you're requesting a rideshare or taxi, enter your destination as the address of a building across the street or someplace else close to your home (not your home address).
- Make sure you're waiting in a safe area—like inside a bar where it's well lit and well populated.
- Never make it obvious that you're waiting for a car service or taxi. If a suspicious character notices a woman milling around, it's easy for them to pull over and claim they're an Uber in an attempt to lure you into the car.

- Make sure you're getting into the right car. Check the app, license plate, make and model, and the name of the driver—and if any of these things don't line up, don't get in.

- Have your choice of personal protection easily accessible to you.

- Never disclose any info to the rideshare driver; strangers don't need to know any personal details about you. Don't share your life story, and don't make small talk that reveals too much about you. If they insist on chatting, you could bring up safe subjects, like how long the person has been driving and whether it's been busy that night. You could also pretend to get a phone call or Facetime a friend if the conversation is making you feel uncomfortable or you don't feel like chatting.

- Lie to survive with your taxi or rideshare driver. You are never traveling alone. You do not live or stay at the location where they drop you off. Your husband or boyfriend will always be at the destination waiting for you.

- Sit behind the driver; this gives you more of an advantage should your gut tell you something feels off. You're out of their direct line of sight and it's harder for them to turn around and see you or get to you.

- Always look at the latch on the door before you get in and make sure that the child lock is not engaged. This pertains mainly to older cars. In newer models, this feature is electronically activated by the driver (scary but important to know).

- Always share your ride information with a trusted family member or friend.

- If you're feeling uncomfortable in a rideshare vehicle, make any excuse needed to end the ride and get out of the car. Say you're about to vomit or you have a personal emergency, or when it's safe to do so, simply unlock the door and get out when you come to a stop sign or stoplight.

- You can also call a male friend or relative and put them on speaker. Tell them exactly where you are and that you'll see them soon.

- A lot of rideshare drivers will have snacks, water, mints, or gum available. No matter how nice the driver may seem, never ingest anything offered inside the vehicle; at the end of the day, you never know what someone is capable of.

- If you encounter a driver who makes you feel unsafe, make sure you report the driver immediately and describe exactly what occurred that made you feel uncomfortable.

Workplace Well-Being

Surviving in Your Office

Americans spend about one-third of their lives at work, and it's a place where we don't have much of a choice whom we spend time with. For that reason, it's super important to keep safety in mind when we're at our jobs (as well as when we're heading to and from work, if we don't work from home).

Shortly after college, I worked briefly with my dad, which often involved attending estate sales. We would typically split up to cover more ground, and at one particular sale I noticed a man who immediately set off alarm bells. Something about him made the hair on the back of my neck stand up. No matter where I went, he always seemed to be lingering nearby. It wasn't outright dangerous, but the unsettling feeling was enough for me to know I wanted to keep my distance.

I reached for my phone to text my dad only to realize I had no cell service. I was on my own to figure a way out. Fortunately, I had been paying attention to the layout of the house, and I was able to slip away through a back stairwell and quietly make my way out of the home. I had car keys with me, so I went straight to the car, got in, and locked the doors.

A few minutes later, my dad—who had obviously been looking for me—spotted me sitting in the car. As soon as he got in, I explained why I'd left, and he immediately knew who I was talking about, describing the man perfectly. Then my dad said, "You're not going to believe this—he must have seen us come in together because he walked up to me and asked, 'How many goats for the girl?'"

We had a good laugh afterward, but the situation was a stark reminder of why it's so important to stay aware of your surroundings, trust your instincts, and always know your exits.

Oh, and if you were wondering what my dad said back, it was, "There aren't enough goats in the world."

What follows are some important reminders about how to stay safe when you're at work, whether that's in an office, a school, a store, a coffee shop, or anywhere else. If some of these tips don't apply to your particular type of job, that's okay—simply take what *does* apply and leave the rest.

> **KEEP YOUR PERSONAL LIFE SEPARATE FROM YOUR WORK LIFE—AND DON'T OVERSHARE.** Trust needs to be earned, not given freely. While it's great to build connections at work, be mindful of how much you share about your personal life until you truly know and trust someone. In a perfect world, we could trust everyone we encounter, but unfortunately that's not the reality. Keeping some separation between your work and home life is important—not just for maintaining boundaries but for your safety as well. You never know who might be paying closer attention than you'd like.
>
> Additionally, set clear boundaries with anyone who seems overly interested or makes you uncomfortable. If there's a coworker who frequently flirts with you or brings up inap-

propriate topics, be direct and assertive. Let them know their behavior isn't welcome. For instance, if they ask a personal question you'd rather not answer, you can say, "I don't feel comfortable discussing that" or "I need to be honest—your question is inappropriate." If their behavior persists, speak to a manager about it. And remember, it's best to avoid sharing personal details like where you live or intimate aspects of your daily life with colleagues, especially those who make you uneasy.

❱ **KNOW YOUR OFFICE LAYOUT AND EMERGENCY EXITS AND PLANS.** This might seem rudimentary, but it's important to have a firm grasp on where all the nearest stairwells and emergency exits are located on your floor. Also, pay attention to fire and safety drills—if the time comes, you'll need that information.

❱ **KEEP YOUR WORKSPACE TIDY.** If there's a fire or other type of emergency, you'll want to be able to easily make your way to the closest exit. This means your workspace should be neat, tidy, and uncluttered, especially on the floor. Clutter can hide potential hazards, such as spills, sharp objects, or tools that could cause you to trip or fall.

Preparation Is Key

If you want to play it extra safe at work, consider having the following items in your drawers or near your desk. At the very least, know where your workplace stores its first-aid and safety equipment, such as fire extinguishers. Additional items you might consider for your own personal use include:

- Fire blanket

- First-aid kit
- Anti-choking device (see A List of Safety Tools on page 207)
- Personal safety device (if it's legal and authorized in your state and company)

❱ SECURE YOUR WORKSPACE. Avoid leaving sensitive documents or personal information out in the open. Not to sound paranoid, but you simply don't know what your coworkers are capable of. If you have a drawer that locks, keep your sensitive documents and materials inside that drawer, and be sure to stash your purse, gym bag, and other belongings out of sight whenever possible. If you have your own office and it has a lock, always lock it up when you're leaving for the night. It's not a bad idea to lock it anytime you're not using it, for that matter.

❱ KEEP YOUR BAG AT YOUR DESK IN A LOCKED DRAWER, IF POSSIBLE. Your purse includes important items like your ID, cash, and any medications you might need on a regular basis. In the event of an emergency—like a fire, earthquake, or (God forbid) a workplace shooting—you'll want to be able to grab the important stuff in one fast motion.

❱ USE PRIVACY SETTINGS ON SOCIAL MEDIA. Your coworkers don't need to see posts about your day-to-day routine, where you live, and your personal life. Most social media sites and apps have settings that allow you to choose who sees the information you post (for example, the "close friends" setting on Instagram or the privacy filters in your Facebook settings).

Your life is not your colleagues' business, and unless you're legitimately close friends with them, it's safer to preserve your privacy.

- **MAINTAIN YOUR DIGITAL PRIVACY ON YOUR WORK COMPUTER.** To play it safe, it's best not to sign in to your personal email or social media accounts from work. When you do that, you're using a device that's not fully under your control—it's managed by your employer. What does this mean? Your company could potentially track your activity, view the websites you're visiting, and possibly even record your keystrokes. Anything you type or read, including personal emails, could technically be seen or saved by your IT department.

  Another issue is security. Office networks often have strict security controls to keep their data safe. But if you sign in to your personal accounts from the same computer, you could accidentally introduce security risks. For instance, if your personal email gets hacked, malware could spread to your employer's network.

  If you're reading or responding to personal emails on a work device, sensitive information could be exposed if IT does system checks or if you forget to log out. If you *do* decide to sign in to those sites, be aware of the risks, and make sure you're taking measures to log out of them before you head home for the day.

- **DON'T WEAR YOUR WORK UNIFORM OR YOUR OFFICE BADGE OUTSIDE OF WORK.** Don't display your badge or lanyard in the car; in fact, don't display anything with your name or other personal information on it. Make sure any clues about your workplace won't be visible for the outside world to see. For instance, if you're a nurse and you wear scrubs every day, wear normal clothes to and from work and change into and out of your scrubs at the office. (This is extra important if your scrubs state the name of the hospital or office where you work.) Things happen, and if you get into a weird exchange with a stranger out in the real world, it's best that they don't know where to find you.

> **LET A FRIEND, PARTNER, OR FAMILY MEMBER KNOW IF YOU'RE WORKING LATE OR ON AN UNUSUAL SCHEDULE.** Make sure somebody knows where you are—especially if you're heading out for an early-morning, late-night, or overnight shift. Shoot that person a quick message about when you're leaving and when you expect to be back. It's a simple way to boost your personal safety, and it gives you both a sense of security. You can also text them when you arrive at work and again when you're heading home.

> **CONTROL WHO FOLLOWS YOU OUT OF YOUR WORKPLACE.** If you're leaving the building alone, and you spot someone outside who gives you a bad vibe, go back inside and wait it out for a few minutes. Similarly, if a fellow employee who creeps you out tries to follow you or walk you out, change your plan and say you need to run back to your desk to grab something. Remember, lie to survive!

Real-World Safety Story

Years ago when I was in retail, I sometimes worked a night shift. As a manager, I closed the store, typically with another manager. One time it was rainy and late in the evening. Walking out of the department store with a male coworker, we both popped open our umbrellas. We reached the large, empty parking lot, then headed in different directions to our cars. I unlocked my car door and quickly pulled in my umbrella.

Like always, I immediately locked my door when I got in my car. I was busy folding up the umbrella when, within seconds, I heard someone trying to open my driver's-side door. I thought it was my coworker—the windows were wet from rain so I didn't have a clear view. As they leaned in while trying to lift the handle, I realized it was not my coworker, and I panicked. I hit my horn and put my bright headlights on, and the guy ran up the hill in front of my car. I drove home a mess.

The next day, I reported the incident to my employer. I was told they were on the lookout for a guy who had attacked a girl in that parking lot. I am so thankful I locked my car doors that night.

—Jill

THE TAKEAWAY
Lock your doors the moment you get into your car, house, dorm, wherever— this must be immediate.

- **TRY NOT TO BE TOO PREDICTABLE IN THE ROUTE YOU TAKE TO AND FROM WORK.** It's easy to live on autopilot, but try to mix it up if, for instance, you start seeing the same person at the same time who gives you a weird gut feeling. If you usually drive to work alone, try going with a friend, taking the bus, or walking instead. Who knows—you may spot a great new restaurant while you're at it! Also, if you drive, be sure to park in different spots (and different parking lots) if possible. It's also helpful to use different entrances at work if you have the option to do so. Generally, just try to be aware of what's going on around you—you know the drill.

> **IF YOU MUST LEAVE WORK LATE**... as an extra layer of security, it's a smart move to have a friend or family member meet you as you're heading out. Think of it as a twist on the classic buddy system.
>
> If you can't swing that, why not ask a friendly coworker to hang out for a bit while you finish up? Sure, they might be itching to get home, but you never know—they might be up for a quick chat or some company while you close up shop. Don't hesitate to ask someone you trust.

> **IF YOU'RE BEING HARASSED ON THE JOB**... Harassment, which includes unwelcome behaviors such as offensive jokes, name-calling, sexual advances, threats, or intimidation, isn't always tied to sex or gender. It can also target race, religion, age, disability, sexual orientation, and more. While addressing it may feel uncomfortable, if you're experiencing harassment at work—no matter the reason—it's important to take the following steps:

- **ACKNOWLEDGE IT FOR WHAT IT IS.** Admit to yourself that you're being harassed. Don't dismiss it or minimize it; what's happening is not okay, and it shouldn't be brushed under the rug.

- **DOCUMENT THE HARASSMENT.** Compile any emails or text messages that discuss the incidents that took place. Write down the details of what happened, with whom, and when—clear recordkeeping is super important.

- **FIND OUT IF YOUR WORKPLACE HAS AN ANTI-HARASSMENT POLICY.** This might be listed on the website or in your employee manual. If there is a policy, follow the steps it lists to report the harassment.

- **REPORT IT.** I know it's not always easy or practical to do this—and it can have career repercussions—but it's important to report it. (At some companies, it's actually mandatory.) This could be with HR, your supervisor, or another department, depending on your individual place of work and its policies around harassment. If you don't feel comfortable reporting the behavior to anyone at work, you can also report harassment directly to the US Equal Employment Opportunity Commission. Consider meeting with an employment attorney.

) **WHAT IF IT'S YOUR BOSS WHO MAKES YOU UNCOMFORTABLE?** If your supervisor's actions or words are causing discomfort, there are steps you can take to address the situation:

- **TALK TO YOUR BOSS ABOUT YOUR CONCERNS.** This is a judgment call—if you feel your boss would be responsive to you expressing concerns in a calm and respectful manner, by all means try it. If not, don't. Clearly explain what actions or behaviors have made you uncomfortable and set a boundary to maintain professionalism. For example, you might say, "Thanks for meeting with me. I want to address an important issue—some recent interactions between us have made me uncomfortable [describe the interaction], and I feel it's necessary to establish a clear boundary to ensure a productive and respectful work environment. I value our working relationship and hope we can move forward with mutual respect and professionalism."

- **ESTABLISH CLEAR BOUNDARIES.** Outline what you will and won't accept in the workplace, and explain your expectations going forward. Stay calm and composed, avoiding an accusatory tone. Simply state the facts and your needs.

- **TALK TO HR IF NEEDED.** If your boss dismisses your concerns or their behavior doesn't change, arrange a meeting with HR to escalate the issue.

- **MANAGE YOUR ANXIETY.** Coping with a difficult supervisor can be stressful. Establish a self-care routine to help manage your anxiety, and consider therapy as a healthy outlet.

- **CONSIDER A NEW ROLE.** If the situation doesn't improve, explore opportunities to work under a different manager or start searching for a new job. You can also ask HR about internal openings that may allow for a change.

❭ **SHOULD YOU USE YOUR REAL NAME ON YOUR NAME TAG?** If you work in a public-facing role, such as a server, receptionist, or barista, your employer may require you to wear a name tag. However, I generally advise against sharing your real name, even if it's a common one, for privacy and safety reasons. Consider your own comfort level with this policy. If you feel safer not using your real name, try using an alias instead. The goal is to protect your privacy and minimize the risk of a disgruntled customer looking you up online—or worse, stalking you.

❭ **IF YOU'RE BEING STALKED BY A CUSTOMER. . .** talk to your manager about the situation so they can address it directly. This includes regular customers who hang around during your shifts or make unwelcome advances. Your manager should advocate for you and take steps to ensure your safety, such as speaking to the customer or, if necessary, banning them from the premises. If the issue persists and no other solutions work, you can request a shift change as a last resort. And remember, if you ever feel unsafe, it's always okay to call 911.

> **IF YOU'RE PREGNANT OR NURSING OR PLANNING TO START A FAMILY...** familiarize yourself with the accommodations for using a breast pump in your workplace and the laws in your state that show what you're legally entitled to. Under the Fair Labor Standards Act, most nursing mothers are entitled to reasonable break time and a private space that is not a bathroom to pump breast milk. If your workplace doesn't already have appropriate accommodations, speak with your boss about arranging for one.

> **PRIORITIZE YOUR MENTAL HEALTH TO AVOID EMOTIONAL BURNOUT.** Taking care of yourself is essential for your well-being and ensures you can show up as your best self, both personally and professionally. When your mental health is in check, it also positively impacts the people you work with. Follow these suggestions:

- Request time off when needed. Even a day or two—paid or unpaid—can make a substantial difference in recharging and resetting.

- Set boundaries. Maintain a healthy work-life balance, and, as much as possible, avoid emotionally bringing your work home with you.

- Learn to say no. If a coworker asks you to cover their shift and you're already stretched too thin, it's okay to decline. Prioritize your health.

- Take breaks. Step away from your desk or workspace throughout the day whenever possible to refresh your mind—and be sure to take your mandated breaks and lunchtime.

- Practice self-care. This could mean anything from taking a relaxing bath to going for a jog to unwinding with your favorite Netflix series. Do what feels restorative for you.

- Seek professional help if needed. A therapist or counselor can provide valuable support and tools to help you navigate stress and prevent burnout.

❱ **IF YOU EVER HAVE TO FIRE SOMEONE** . . . try to have security or HR present when you're doing it. Most larger companies will have a mandated process for this, but whenever possible, have the conversation in a neutral area—not in your office or workspace. Meeting in a conference room or cafeteria is ideal. Disable the employee's security badge before having a difficult conversation—the last thing you want is an angry, upset, or otherwise disgruntled employee who has easy access to reenter the building. (We've all heard the horror stories, right?) After the termination, make sure security is aware of the situation.

Utilize de-escalation tactics. Use calm language, maintain a serene demeanor, and avoid challenging statements or accusations. Less is more if you need to have one of these hard conversations. Set the person free in a peaceful way (even if they've been a problematic employee). Firing someone is a time to quiet your own ego as well as to forget about things that have happened with the employee in the past—at this point, anything that happened earlier is water under the bridge. Keep the temperature of the conversation cool and fair.

Script It Out

> **LETTING SOMEONE GO**
>
> If you need to fire someone . . .
>
> *Start with a straightforward statement:* "I need to talk to you about your position here."
>
> *Focus on the facts:* "I'm sorry to tell you this, but we're going to have to let you go."
>
> *Acknowledge how tough the situation is and show empathy toward the person (even if you secretly can't stand them!):* "I know this is hard to hear."
>
> *Give them space to ask questions and process what you've said:* "Is there anything you need clarity on?"
>
> *End the conversation respectfully and kindly:* "Again, I know this is difficult news, but I want you to know how much we've valued your contributions here. I wish you the best of luck going forward."
>
> **WHAT NOT TO SAY**
>
> - Don't air a laundry list of grievances or accusations or recap of how they've failed at their job. Don't say: "I was forced to do this given the consistent inadequacy of your work."

- Don't criticize their "fit" for the office or the job. Don't say: "I don't know if you were ever actually the right fit for this role. Blending into the office culture never seemed to come naturally to you."

- Don't discuss their future prospects. Don't say: "I have doubts about your ability to find another position in this field."

- Don't imply that they should have anticipated this turn of events. Don't say: "You should have seen this coming."

Bonus Tips for My Girls Who Babysit (or Nanny)

Babysitting is a common side hustle for women. Here are some tips to keep in mind:

- Take a child safety course before you start working so you'll know infant and child CPR/first aid.

- Do some online digging before working with a new family. Check them out on social media and try to suss out whether it will be a safe and healthy working environment.

- Have a meet and greet before you start working with a new family.

- If they don't already have indoor cameras, ask the family to install some in the public areas of the house. This protects both you and the family by providing transparency and helping prevent misunderstandings.

- Don't let the family leave for the night without sharing the contact info for the nearest hospital, the number for the child's doctor, and a friend or family member's phone number.

- Ask for a medical release form for each child individually so you can take them to the emergency room and get them treated immediately if need be.

- Always make sure someone knows who you're babysitting for, where you'll be, and how long you expect to be there.

- Make sure you're sharing your location with your family or close friends.

- Check in with someone when you're home at the end of the night.

Flying Solo

How to Rock Living on Your Own

Living alone is full of perks—including never having to share the remote, drinking the juice straight out of the carton, keeping things as clean as you like, and not worrying about the position of the toilet seat. Whether you're twenty-two or sixty-two, living alone can be a rite of passage that brings a sense of independence, fun, and freedom. Yet it does come with its own set of risks.

I'd never advise a woman not to live alone—I've done it (and loved it) in various cities around the United States: Las Vegas, Albuquerque, and Chicago, to name a few. But I do advise them to approach it smartly. Remember: Live aware and live empowered, but don't live in fear.

) **ALWAYS LOCK YOUR DOORS.** This suggestion might seem obvious, but always—always—LOCK YOUR DOORS. Getting in or out of your car? LOCK YOUR DOORS. Entering or leaving your home? LOCK YOUR DOORS. This needs to become habitual. If you're not already doing so, start now. Even if you're just running out of your house to grab something from your car or taking the dog around the block, lock the door behind you. Why? Because you never know who's hanging around, potentially watching and waiting to seize on a vulnerable moment. Don't give them one!

- **IF YOU HAVE A GARAGE,** make sure to manually lock the door, as it adds an extra layer of protection, preventing it from being forced open or bypassed electronically. Manually locking your garage door involves engaging a physical locking mechanism, such as a sliding deadbolt or latch. These are typically on both sides of the garage door. This is especially important if you're leaving for a trip, or if you have a power outage, or if you must evacuate in an emergency.

- **INSTALL AN ALARM SYSTEM.** A reliable security system will enhance your sense of safety, whether you're at home or away. The addition of a two-way doorbell camera is another smart step to consider.

- **LIGHT IT UP.** Install motion-activated lighting around your home and ensure your indoor spaces are well lit. Outdoor lighting helps you see who's approaching or entering your property, while indoor lighting signals that the house is occupied, discouraging would-be intruders. Criminals prefer easy, unguarded targets, so keeping your home well lit can act as a strong deterrent. Adding motion-sensor cameras and floodlights can provide a clear visual of anyone lurking nearby, enhancing your security even further.

- **ADD EXTRA SECURITY TO YOUR SLIDING GLASS DOORS AND WINDOWS.** Sliding glass doors are notoriously vulnerable to break-ins.

I would know—when I was in college, I came back from a break to find leaves inside my apartment. I felt a breeze wafting in and found my sliding glass open by about three feet. Someone had clearly been inside my apartment. I ran outside and immediately called 911, and within five minutes, officers were at my front door. They cleared the house and took down all necessary details, but we never figured out who had broken in. When my dad got wind of this, his exact words were, "You're going to Home Depot and getting a dowel rod." Installing a dowel rod can significantly enhance sliding doors' security. Measure your sliding door (or window) and visit a home improvement or hardware store. An employee can cut a rod to the exact size you need (if you're handy, you can do this yourself). Once placed on the track, the dowel rod makes it nearly impossible to open the door from the outside, providing a simple yet effective barrier.

- **GET TO KNOW YOUR NEIGHBORS.** Having a reliable neighbor (who is safety-conscious like you!) watch your home while you're away can provide valuable peace of mind. Developing a strong relationship with at least one close neighbor means you can look out for each other. They'll notify you if they spot anything unusual, fostering a safer and more secure community.

- **GIVE A FRIEND A SPARE KEY.** Give a spare key to a friend, family member, neighbor, or someone else you trust in case you accidentally get locked out or you lose your copy. No matter what, do not hide a key under your welcome mat or inside a fake rock, as criminals are well aware of these strategies.

- **MIND YOUR GARBAGE.** Never place anything in your trash that could draw unwanted attention, such as apparel, jewelry, or high-end electronics (think a big, expensive TV or a box or bag with a designer label on it). You'd be surprised at the lengths some criminals will go to scout out a potential target. Carefully and discreetly dispose of anything tied to high-value items—especially those that contain personal information.

- **HAVE SOMEONE PICK UP YOUR PACKAGES IF YOU'RE OUT OF TOWN.** When you're on vacation, don't let mail or packages accumulate outside your home; this is a dead giveaway that you're out of town. Don't make it easy for people to spot that you aren't there; instead, ask a trusted neighbor or friend to collect your mail and pick up packages for you while you're away. Don't give out info about your travel dates—or any intel that your home will be vacant—to *anyone* except a close friend or neighbor. You can also request that the post office temporarily stop your mail service until you get back.

- **STAY IN THE LOOP WITH YOUR NEIGHBORHOOD.** Pay attention to crime in your area. Read your city newspaper and local websites. Join neighborhood Facebook groups and a neighborhood-watch app. These apps alert residents to real-time happenings and allow users to share incidents of their own.

- **HAVE A NIGHTLY CHECK-IN BUDDY.** Choose a trusted friend or family member to be your check-in person. Plan a specific time each night to call or text them to confirm you're home safe. If you don't check in as scheduled, they'll know something might be wrong and can take action.

- **NEVER MAKE IT KNOWN THAT YOU LIVE ALONE.** Don't tell strangers you live alone. Whether at a party, in a rideshare, or anywhere else, act like you live with a male partner or male roommates (see page 109). A woman who lives alone is unfortunately perceived as more vulnerable, and a simple lie to survive can fend off unwanted interest or attention.

Real-World Safety Story

I was sitting on my couch when I heard a knock at my door. I went to my window and saw a black truck with Massachusetts license plates (I live in Pennsylvania). There was a man behind the wheel, and another man standing by the truck. At first I ignored the knock, hoping the person would go away. The person kept knocking, so I said, "What?" The person said they needed me to open the door. I said, "I don't open the door!" The person again said, "Ma'am, I need you to open the door!"

I told them I was on the phone with the cops (I wasn't really). Then the person said, "Ha, I *am* the cops! I'm Officer Jake Lance." So I dialed 911 and told the dispatcher that the person outside said he was a cop. The dispatcher told me to ask the man what department he was from. The man outside said, "Pittsburgh." The dispatcher on the phone said, "He's not a cop.' Then the man said, "I need you to open the door! I'm counting down . . . ten, nine, eight, seven . . ."

I told the dispatcher that the man was counting down and that I thought he was going to break my door in. When he got to number one, the dispatcher told me they'd arrived and were in my driveway. I came to find out later that the men in the truck were traveling up the East Coast, stealing from people. The state trooper believed they were trying to perform a "distracted theft."

—Tamara

THE TAKEAWAY:

Never open your door to anyone you don't know or aren't expecting, and if need be, call 911 immediately.

Never open your door

- If you're not expecting anyone, never open your door—even for delivery drivers. I personally never open my door to *anyone* I don't know unless I'm expecting a package that I know needs a signature and I'm aware of which carrier it's coming from. People have been known to pose as uniformed delivery drivers to lure you into opening the door so they can gain access to your home.

- If you have one, use a camera with two-way audio to talk to a delivery driver: "Thanks so much; please leave the package there and I'll have my husband grab it."

- Don't stand right behind the door. This can put you in a dangerous position should a malicious individual forcefully attempt to break in.

- Some individuals use deceptive tactics, like the sound of a crying baby or claims of a "lost child" to trick you into opening your door. If you hear a baby crying or a child approaches your home seeking help, stay inside and assess the situation from a safe vantage point. Avoid stepping outside—instead, call 911 immediately.

Script It Out

IF SOMEONE KNOCKS AT YOUR DOOR AND ASKS FOR HELP

If someone shows up claiming that they need immediate help, remember—don't open the door. You could be opening yourself up to a home invasion. Instead, talk to them through the door or through your doorbell camera. Your best bet is to say something like "I'm so sorry, I can't open the door, but I'm calling 911 for you." If they continue pressing, tell them, "The police will be here momentarily."

- **ORDERING FOOD.** Whether you're ordering from Uber Eats or Instacart or directly from a restaurant, never use your real name to place your order—use a man's name. Have fun with it—try picking the most stereotypically "masculine" name you can think of, like Rex or Bo (because hey, why not?). Also, always choose contact-free delivery so the delivery person doesn't need to see you face-to-face or get a glimpse inside your home. There may be persistent drivers who don't follow your directions, so use the messaging app to communicate and reiterate that they can leave the food at the door. You can even throw in something like "thanks, man" to really sell the idea that you're a dude.

- **IF YOU HAVE A TRADESPERSON IN THE HOME.** When hiring outside workers like handy people, plumbers, or painters, it's important to be cautious since you can never be entirely sure who you're inviting into your home. Before they arrive, secure personal items such as jewelry, checkbooks, prescriptions, calendars, or bank statements, and remain alert while they're on the job.

Real-World Safety Story

About fifteen years ago, we hired a contractor to remodel our home. Subcontractors were in and out of our home for weeks. All went as planned and we were pleased with the work.

Approximately six months after the job was completed, while I was home alone, my doorbell rang. My office faces the front of our home and I saw one of the carpenters walking up our driveway. I put my headset on and walked to my front door. I have a picture window next to my front door and never open my door to anyone I'm not expecting. I slid the window open and said, "Can I help you?" The man reminded me that he was one of the carpenters on our recent remodel and wanted to "check the back doors." I asked if there was a problem and he said no, "I just really liked the quality and I need to check the serial numbers."

I immediately felt the hair on my neck and arms stand up. I pointed to my headset and then held my finger up. I then said, literally to no one, "Honey, I have one of the carpenters here and he wants the serial number from the back doors." Then I looked at my watch and said, "'Okay great, honey, see you in five."

I apologized to the man at my door and said, "My husband is calling your boss now, so you should call him for any further questions." I shut and locked the window prior to going back to my office. I immediately called my husband—I was so freaked out! The man never returned. My husband called his boss, who told him this particular carpenter actually picked up and delivered the doors to our job site! We changed all our locks that day.

—Jamie

THE TAKEAWAY:

Lie to survive.

> **THE FAUX MALE "ROOMMATE."** Even if you're single, pretend you're not, at least when other people are around. If a worker is in your home, be sure to mention your husband or boyfriend so they don't think you live alone. To make the ruse even more sophisticated, try keeping a pair of men's shoes at the entryway of your home, and hang an oversize men's coat in a visible location. Basically, pretend a man lives with you. You'd be surprised how much this can help deter someone from shady activity.

> **USE AN ALIAS.** There's rarely a reason to use your real name for interactions in a public setting, such as ordering at a coffee shop or picking up food. When I lived alone in Chicago, I used an alias at the cafe down the street. It wasn't just about keeping strangers from knowing my name, it was also a layer of safety. If, God forbid, someone tried to follow me home and asked my door attendant for "Minnie," they would respond, "I don't know of a Minnie that lives here" and send them away. Door attendants should be trained not to answer personal questions about building residents, but that doesn't necessarily mean they'll follow protocol.

> **DON'T STATE PERSONAL DETAILS OUT LOUD.** For example, when picking up a prescription or checking into a hotel, protect your privacy by handing over your ID instead of stating your name and address aloud. You can also write your information on a piece of paper to share it quietly. Be sure to ask the staff not to repeat your personal details out loud to ensure that your information stays private.

> **GETTING CASH OUT.** One of the easiest ways to make yourself a target is by holding a cash envelope in plain sight after an ATM withdrawal. It may seem harmless, but to the wrong

person, it's an open invitation. Always practice situational awareness. As soon as you receive cash, tuck it away in an internal pocket of your purse or jacket—somewhere only you know. Don't advertise what you're carrying.

> **DON'T POST IN REAL TIME ON SOCIAL MEDIA.** As mentioned on page 76, posting in real time on social media is one of the easiest ways we can open ourselves up to trouble. Sharing our actual location in an Instagram story or checking in somewhere on Facebook can lead someone with nefarious intentions right to you. Never make yourself easy to find. If you want to tag your local watering hole or the new restaurant you visited on Saturday night, do it after the fact, not while you're physically there. By the way, Kim Kardashian also follows this advice—no one is too famous or too well protected to be above simple safety tips.

Exercising Safely

When I lived alone, anytime I went out for a run or a walk I would text a friend or family member with the time I was leaving and my planned route. I also made sure to let them know how long I'd be gone and that I'd call or text them when I got home safely. Make sure you do the same! According to a 2023 Adidas study,[*] 92 percent of 4,500 women surveyed reported that they worry about their safety when they go out for a run, so make sure you stay on top of the following precautions:

---

[*] "New Adidas Study Finds 92% of Women Are Concerned for Their Safety When They Go for a Run," Adidas, March 10, 2023, https://news.adidas.com/running/new-adidas-study-finds-92-of-women-are-concerned-for-their-safety-when-they-go-for-a-run/s/c318f69e-7575-4ced-bbf3-9db6d2ab1642.

- Make sure you're aware of your surroundings. Situational awareness is crucial.
- Always keep your head out of your phone, and if you use earbuds, keep one ear free so you can hear everything around you.
- Walk with your head high, a strong posture, and a sense of purpose.
- Carry a form of personal protection, as well as a personal key chain alarm, and be sure to keep these items easily accessible and not buried in your bag or fanny pack. A distracted person is an easy target, and your goal is to never be one.

❭ **WATCH OUT FOR AIRTAGS.** People with questionable motives have been known to attach an AirTag or other tracking device to victims' belongings or vehicles, so always be cautious about who has access to your things, whether you're traveling or staying local. It's a good habit to empty your purse or bag when you return home from a trip or outing to ensure that no tracking device or other unfamiliar item has been added. Keep an eye out for anything unusual attached to your vehicle. If you discover a tracker that doesn't belong to you, disable it, bring it into the police station, and file a report. To disable an AirTag, simply press down on it, turn it counterclockwise, and remove the battery.

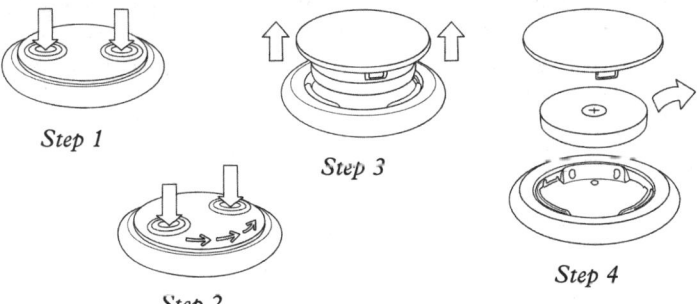

Step 1

Step 2

Step 3

Step 4

Roommates

The Pros and Cons

Beyond the issue of safety, choosing a person with whom you'll be sharing your personal space for an extended period of time affects every aspect of your life. Here are some ways to think about the decision:

Pros

- You share the rent, so you can potentially afford a nicer place with more amenities.
- There's safety in numbers.
- It can be comforting having someone else in the house.
- A roommate can pick up/sign for your packages when you're out of town.
- You have a built-in check-in person to share your plans with—someone who will notice any deviations from your daily routine.
- If you have pets, you may have a built-in pet-sitter, eliminating the need to give another person access to your house.
- Should a dangerous situation arise, you have live-in backup.

Cons

- It's impossible to *truly* know someone, so don't move in with anyone unless you feel extremely confident that they're trustworthy. If your roommate isn't on the same page safety-wise, they could make your home less secure; if they have parties, bring home strangers, leave doors unlocked, or leave windows open, it's opening both of you up to unnecessary risks.
- You have less control over what happens in your home. Your roommate may engage in activities that you don't participate in,

such as using illegal substances, drinking heavily, smoking, or other behaviors that you may not be comfortable with.

Questions to Ask to Vet Potential Roommates

- What does your daily routine look like? (You'll want to make sure the two of you align on a day-to-day level.)
- How do you handle conflict?
- What were your past roommate experiences like?
- What's your outlook on keeping our living space safe?
- What's your stance on drug and alcohol use at home?
- How do you handle emergency situations?
- Do you own a firearm? If so, how do you store it?
- Do you have a romantic partner who would be spending time here too?

Additionally, it's always best to do your own homework—Google them, look up their social media, and get a read on what this person is like. If you have any mutual friends, talk to the person who knows them and try to make sure everything they say checks out. If you notice any story inconsistencies through that mutual friend or while talking with the person directly, that's a red flag. You can even do a background check. At the end of the day, it's a judgment call—if you feel good about living with this person, trust your gut.

> **WHAT IF SOMEONE FOLLOWS YOU HOME?** If you suspect you're being followed, never head home. Stay vigilant and practice situational awareness so you can quickly recognize and respond to potential threats. If you're driving, call 911 immediately and

proceed directly to the nearest fire or police station. If you're on foot, look for a store, restaurant, or any crowded, well-lit area. These actions will significantly enhance your safety.

If you realize you've been followed after arriving home, act quickly. Use your phone's emergency SOS function (if available) to alert emergency services immediately. If the individual approaches you aggressively, create distance and defend yourself with pepper gel or spray (or the self-defense tool you feel comfortable using). In moments like these, hesitation is not an option. Scream, yell, and make as much noise as possible to draw attention to yourself and let those around you know you need help. Your priority is survival, so do whatever it takes to protect yourself.

Set Up a Strong Room

A strong room or safe room is a place where you can barricade yourself inside and buy time while you wait for police to arrive—a bedroom, closet with a door, or a bathroom could work (ideally one with no windows and a deadbolt). Keep a form of personal protection in the designated room to defend yourself should you need to do so.

> **WHAT TO DO IN A HOME INVASION.** If you're the target of a home invasion, grab your cell phone and call 911 while simultaneously moving to your strong room. This is another instance where it's important to have played the "what if" game (as discussed on page 25). In a home invasion situation, you'll want to have a loose plan already mapped out in your head;

your strategies need to be premeditated so you can spring into action.

> **WHAT TO DO IF YOUR HOME GETS BROKEN INTO WHILE YOU'RE OUT?**

If you ever come home and discover your house has been broken into (as you know, I can empathize with this), it's completely natural to feel fear, anger, sadness, or a sense of violation. Those emotions are valid and understandable. At the same time, take comfort in knowing that you weren't there when it happened. Your safety is what matters most. In this situation, never go inside by yourself. Leave immediately and call 911. This is where having cameras and a home security system can make all the difference. Being able to review footage gives you crucial insight into what happened and can help law enforcement with its investigation.

If afterward you feel unsafe staying in your home, there's nothing wrong with asking a friend or family member if you can spend a couple of nights at their place.

Remember, while the odds of becoming a crime victim are slim, it can still happen anytime and anywhere. Being in a safe neighborhood, building, or home doesn't guarantee you won't be a target. That's why practicing situational awareness, arming yourself with knowledge, and implementing layers of safety, like carrying self-defense tools, are so important. These habits aren't about living in fear; they're about being prepared, confident, and empowered to protect yourself and your loved ones.

Adventures in Traveling Alone

How to Jet-Set Safely

Traveling alone can be incredibly fun and meaningful. It builds your confidence, allows you to meet new people and see the world, and helps you learn to appreciate your own likes, dislikes, strengths, and interests in a whole new way. But it can also carry risks, especially if you're a woman, as unfair as that is. For this reason, I share a range of ideas on what to do—and not do—when you're traveling on your own or visiting a new place. Though this chapter is geared more toward solo travelers, these tips can apply to any kind of travel.

The most important tip I can give, and one I've mentioned before, is to practice situational awareness wherever you go. Anytime you arrive at a new location, take a moment to pause and get a sense of your surroundings. Identify the exits, observe the people nearby, and assess the overall vibe. If something feels "off," or your gut is giving you a warning, don't ignore it. Trust yourself and consider leaving for a safer environment. Your instincts are often your best guide. (Practicing situational awareness in your daily life will make it second nature for when you're traveling—a very good thing!)

❯ **CHECK YOUR BAGGAGE FOR FORBIDDEN ITEMS.** People have faced serious consequences when airport officials have found items like stray bullets or weapon parts that were accidentally overlooked in their luggage while traveling. This highlights how crucial it is to double-check your bags before any trip, domestic or international. Something as small as a single bullet can lead to legal trouble (like being detained or arrested, and facing serious jail time in a foreign country). This might disrupt your travel plans, to say the least. *Always* take the extra time to ensure your luggage is completely clear of *anything* that could raise red flags.

❯ **DON'T GET CAUGHT OFF-GUARD IN A NEW CITY—WHEN POSSIBLE, PLAN YOUR TRIP IN ADVANCE.** Typically, when it comes to travel, there are two kinds of people—those who plan everything out in great detail in advance and those who like to wing it. I want to empower both types of people, and for those who are a bit more spontaneous, know you can have your freedom while still prioritizing your safety.

Regardless of which type of person you are, make sure you have a solid game plan for your trip ahead of time, so you're never stuck with limited options. If you're an anti-planner, you're still going to want to do at least a little bit of advance research so you'll have the lay of the land and feel comfortable in your new destination. The more prepared you are, the less likely you'll find yourself dealing with unexpected circumstances.

- Share your itinerary with a friend, partner, or relative before you leave—even if it's a last-minute itinerary—

including your accommodations, important phone numbers, and addresses.

- Plan to have a buddy back home with whom you'll check in daily. If they don't hear from you by the agreed-upon time, they'll know something is wrong. If this were to happen, your friend should contact the nearest US embassy or consulate or American Citizen Services to request a welfare check. Share your phone location with family and close friends back home so they can see where you are in real time.

- Again, never post in real time on social media. This is not only so you can avoid people knowing that your home is currently vacant, you also never want to give a foreign stranger the ability to be able to find you based on your most recent Instagram story. Post only after you are no longer at that specific location.

- Watch out for pickpockets. Keep your valuables in a zippered compartment that you can wear on the front of your body (for example, a coat, a cross-body bag, or a fanny pack); don't keep anything important where it's easily accessible on your back.

- If you are ever approached by an individual with an unsolicited offer to sell you something, respond with a polite but assertive "no, thank you" and continue walking. This may be harder for some people than for others—consider it a practice in assertiveness—but keep those feet moving.

❱ **HOW TO MAKE YOURSELF THE LEAST IDEAL TARGET.** I've mentioned before that most criminals are looking for easy targets, and it's true. The less you fulfill the "ideal target" checklist, the less appealing you are. Keep these things in mind while you're traveling.

- How you walk, talk, and carry yourself plays a huge role in helping you avoid being targeted. Always be mindful of your stride and your posture. Walk with confidence, with your head up, and with a purpose; you have places to go and people to see, and you know exactly what you're doing—even if you don't. Never allow yourself to be distracted while walking; keep your head out of your phone anytime you're out and about.

- If you need to look at your phone to check a map or respond to a text, step inside a well-populated shop. If that's not an option, scan your surroundings and place your back against a nearby wall. This minimizes your exposure to being approached.

- Strong eye contact and a sense of acknowledgment with the people around you conveys that you're observing any potential threats.

- If you find yourself in a threatening situation, draw as much attention to yourself as possible. Remember, noise is your friend.

- Forgo the expensive jewelry or designer handbags when you're traveling solo, as this can place a target on your back. The goal is to blend in.

Real-World Safety Story

My female coworker and I were on a work trip. We were heading to the elevator to go up to her room to grab our stuff.

The elevator doors were about to close, my coworker had clicked the button to her floor, and a guy slipped in at the last minute. I realized it was a guy from outside on the street who had checked me out.

She asked him which floor he was on, and he pointedly looked at the elevator numbers, saw which one was lit up, and then said the same floor as us. My gut was screaming that something was wrong.

When I'm at home, I carry pepper spray and a small stun gun, but I didn't have those on me since we were traveling. When we were riding up the elevator, I wondered what we were going to do if he tried anything—could we fight this guy? (He was a lot larger than us.)

We got to the fourth floor and he bent down like he was tying his shoe. It seemed like he was waiting for us to get off the elevator first. My gut was screaming, "Do not get off this elevator!"

So I shot my hand out to stop my coworker from getting off and said, "I forgot something down in the lobby. We're going back down."

When we got down to the lobby, we went to the front desk and asked one of the guys there to walk us up to our room. As we were heading up there, I told the front desk manager about the guy, and he said the man wasn't a guest and was actually on their watchlist as he had come into the hotel a few times.

—Alissa

THE TAKEAWAY

Never isolate yourself in a "steel box" with someone who is giving you bad vibes. If you're already on the elevator, do whatever you can to remove yourself from the situation as soon as possible.

Air Travel

Traveling by airplane can often seem routine—but that doesn't mean you should wing it! Here are some tips on how to fly safely:

- Make sure your phone is fully charged before you head to the airport; bring a portable charger as well.

- If you drive and self-park at the airport, remove all personal or valuable items (E-ZPass, cash, registration, house keys, garage door openers, insurance cards, and so on) from your car before locking up and heading in. If this isn't feasible, make sure everything is securely locked away and that nothing is visible from outside the vehicle.

- Don't keep mail or anything else showing your home address in the car. Never store your actual home address in your GPS—instead, use a local gas station or pharmacy. Think how easy a home burglary would be if someone stole your car and the car led them straight to your vacant home.

- Don't forget to lock your car!

- Keep your wallet and phone stashed in an internal pocket of your bag so they're not visible or easily grabbable.

- Hold your license or ID face down when you're waiting in line for security. Your license has your full name and address on it; you do not want people viewing this information. The same applies with your boarding pass, which also has your full name on it.

- Don't leave your items unattended . . . ever.

- If you're using the restroom, avoid putting your purse or bag on a hook located on the back of the door, especially if the hook is positioned near the top of the door. Someone can reach over the door, grab your purse, and run out of the restroom. This happens—in fact, it happened to someone I know!

- Remember, if anyone asks, you're not traveling alone. Say you have friends or family on this flight (they're just sitting in a different section) or that your dad/brothers will be picking you up when you land.

Dos and Don'ts for International Airports

Traveling internationally is exciting, but it also presents a unique set of risks. Don't forget to do the following things to make your international travel experience safe and smooth:

- Make two photocopies of your passport. Leave one at home with a family member or trusted friend and take the other one with you, keeping it in a separate place from your actual passport. If you lose your passport while traveling, having a copy of it can expedite its replacement.

- Do general research about the airport beforehand: How far is it from your hotel? Is it considered safe? Where is your terminal located?

- Prepare for any language barrier by downloading a free language translator app. Test out a few phrases before you go so you'll be prepared when you land.

- Always have your hotel transport arranged in advance. In some destinations, it's common to be approached by people as soon as you step off the plane. They might offer you a ride to your hotel or try to sell you something, like a timeshare. To avoid standing out as an uninformed traveler, be confident, remain polite but assertive, and don't let anyone pressure you, especially if it entails getting into a vehicle with a stranger.

- Add at least an hour to your airport travel time so you're not rushed or overly stressed.

Script It Out

DODGING THE UNSOLICITED TAXI DRIVER

You're in an unfamiliar airport in a new country, you're exhausted, and before you can even get your bearings, a man approaches you and says: "Need a ride? Let me grab your bags. Come with me, I'm cheaper than the taxi line." How do you respond? Firmly put a hand on your bags and say, "No, thank you, my transportation is taken care of already." If they keep pushing or offer you a special deal, get moving and assertively say, "I'm not interested, thanks anyway." Then quickly walk away. Being in a new environment, with a stranger in your face, is super uncomfortable—so having a response ready can help you handle that pressure and sense of urgency.

Real-World Safety Story

As a twenty-something woman, I was visiting our family beach house in a small beach town. My mom and her friend who lived there had warned me there was a creepy man they nicknamed "the Pervert" whom they'd witnessed hitting on women of all ages alone at the beach. He would always start the conversation by asking, "Are you local?"

I didn't have anyone to go with me, so I went to the beach by myself. Even though I knew I risked an encounter with him, I wasn't going to let the Pervert keep me from the beach. While relaxing on my towel and reading a book in my bikini, a man came over and asked, "Are you local?" I politely made up a story that I was a college student and needed to finish reading my book for a class, so I couldn't chat with him anymore. He left.

About twenty minutes later, he came back with a book in his hand. He told me he went to the library so he could read with me. I remained calm, cool, and collected, even though I felt vulnerable and unsafe. Again, I politely made up that I had to leave for class. I left the beach the opposite way I came and walked a zigzag route back to the beach house, frequently checking that he was not following.

About a week later, he was arrested for the rape of a woman in the house right next door to ours.

—Anonymous

THE TAKEAWAY

Lie to survive. De-escalation and removing yourself from an unsafe situation as swiftly and safely as possible is the goal.

Hotel Safety

Checking into a hotel involves disclosing quite a bit of personal information to people you don't know. If you go in with a game plan (as always, preparation is key), you'll be able to better protect yourself and your personal details. When you're checking into a hotel:

- Never say any of your personal information out loud.
- Always ask for two keys and say that your husband or boyfriend will be joining you soon. Remember, lie to survive!
- Make sure your room number is not spoken out loud if anyone else is nearby—if so, ask for another room. Make sure nobody follows you to your room. If someone does, head straight back to the lobby.
- Read up on the elevator safety tips on page 21.

Maintenance Check

Whether you're on a hotel balcony or cruise ship, always double-check that glass panels are securely in place where they should be. Tragically, there have been cases of children falling to their deaths because of missing window panels. Also, take a moment to ensure that all the windows are locked for added safety.

Keep These Two Hotel Tricks Up Your Sleeve

The "Do Not Disturb Sign" Trick

Catch the corner of the Do Not Disturb sign in your door when you leave the room. If you come back to the door and find the sign hanging straight, you'll know someone has been in your room. Don't enter alone—go get help.

The "Shoe Behind the Door" Trick

This trick involves placing your shoe (or any other object) right behind the door, as close to the door as possible. When you come back into the room, slowly open your door and look to make sure the shoe is exactly where you left it. If the item is in a different position or has been pushed to a place where it's not visible, then same as above—do not enter and call security.

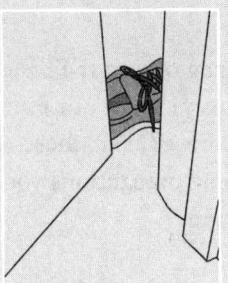 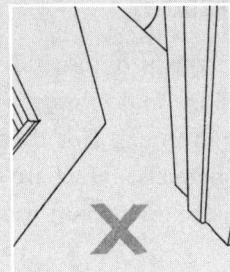 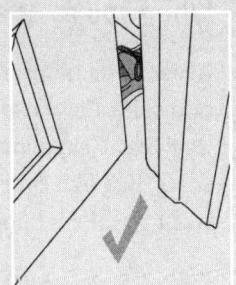

Place a shoe in the doorway.

If it's not exactly where you left it, you're not safe.

If it's in the same spot, you're safe.

If someone knocks on your hotel door in the middle of the night . . .

Never open the door. Depending on the vibe, ignore it, call for help, or talk through the door while pretending you're not alone (you could also call a male friend or family member and put them on speaker—creating the impression that you're not by yourself). If someone is actively trying to break in, call 911 (if you're in the United States) or the front desk to send hotel security.

If someone follows you to your hotel . . .

- Never go to your room.
- Ask the front desk for help.
- Stay where it's well populated—never allow yourself to be isolated. A hotel bar or restaurant is a suitable place to go while you wait for assistance.
- Call 911 if you need to.

When you're at a resort . . .

Most of us go on resort trips to unwind, hang out on the beach, and take a few excursions to do things we can't do in our everyday lives (skydiving, anyone?). But there are risks at these resorts, just like everywhere else. Here are some precautions you'll want to take when you're on a resort vacation:

- Watch your drinks. Don't ever leave your beverage unattended at a bar or by the pool.

- Be mindful anytime you leave the resort to go into town or on an excursion. Do your research. Know where you're going and the risks posed. Is your destination considered safe for tourists?

- Watch your valuables closely. Don't leave your purse, wallet, or phone unattended, and keep them hidden from view as much as possible.

- Don't wear expensive jewelry or carry designer handbags.

- Be mindful of whom you interact with. Don't share unnecessary personal information with anyone.

- Carry only small amounts of cash (just enough to cover your plans for the day).

- Monitor the time—you don't want to miss your return transport and get stranded.

Are your new vacation "friends" actually your friends?

One of the highlights of travel is meeting new people, and there are many opportunities for that when you're exploring new places on your own. But you'll want to be wary, at least a little bit. Follow these simple guidelines when you're mixing and mingling during your travels:

- Get your new buddies' full names and numbers and check them out. Think social media, LinkedIn, and Google. Do they have an online presence? What does that presence say about them? Are they who they say they are?

- Have a burner number that you can use to communicate with people. This will prevent your number from revealing any of your personal information if it's looked up (free apps like Google Voice exist for this in the app store). Your phone number reveals a lot about you, so by taking this simple and free line of defense, you can prevent people from finding personal information about you online.

- Look up their phone number. See if the name matches the name they gave you.
- Don't reveal too much about yourself (e.g., full name, hotel information, etc.) until you get to know them. Leave all the personal details out in the beginning. Be nice but vague.

Safety Tools for Traveling

There are certain weapons you can declare and bring with you in a checked bag, but if you want to keep it simple, here are a few basic things you can bring with you to help serve as personal protection when you're traveling. See A List of Safety Tools on page 207 for more details on each device.

> **A DOORSTOP ALARM FOR YOUR HOTEL ROOM.** One of my favorite travel hacks is bringing a battery-powered doorstop alarm with me anytime I travel.

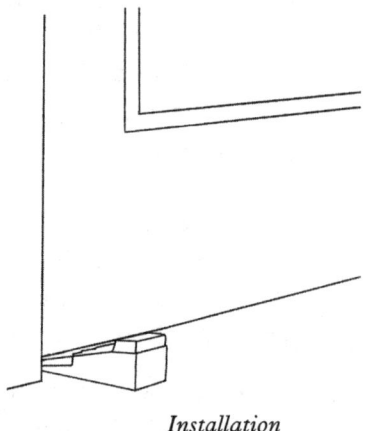

Installation

ADVENTURES IN TRAVELING ALONE

> **A SECURITY BAR.** This universal option is a great tool to travel with.

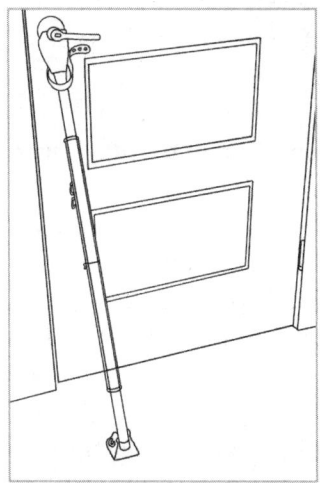
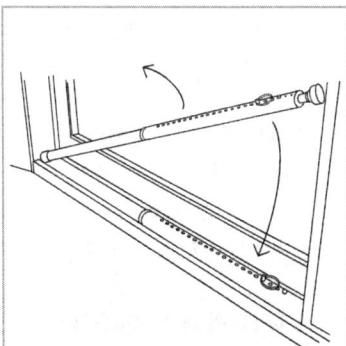

> **PORTABLE STEEL DOOR LOCK.** These cheap, portable door locks serve as enhanced protection for your hotel room door.

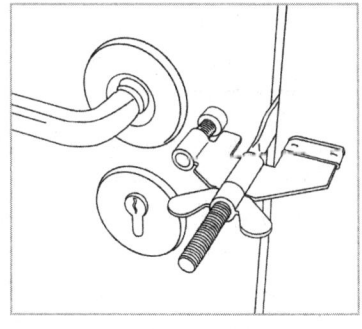

Positioning

- **PEPPER SPRAY OR GEL**, if legal where you're going, can be packed in your checked luggage. Be sure to follow Transportation Security Agency regulations on how it must be stored. Note that some airlines simply may not permit this device at all, so check before leaving home.

- **A TACTICAL PEN** can always go in your checked bag; this is used as a last-resort sharp force weapon.

- **A PERSONAL KEY CHAIN ALARM** is also great to have on you at all times. These can go through security at an airport (I've never had mine taken), but be sure not to accidentally set it off at the airport or on the plane.

- **A CARBON MONOXIDE DETECTOR** can be used in your hotel or Airbnb.

- **A CAR ESCAPE TOOL**, which can go in your checked bag, is a great option to have in the event that you rent a car or use a taxi or rideshare while you're traveling.

Charger Safety

The FBI is advising against the use of public phone charging stations in order to protect devices from potential malicious software. They recommend carrying your own charger and USB cable and using a standard electrical outlet rather than charging through a public USB port (see more on page 178 about using electronics safely). Also, never connect to public Wi-Fi unless you have a VPN. Hackers can intercept any online activity—they can steal your personal data, including your bank information, credit card number, social media passwords, and more. A VPN encrypts all of your online activity.

Beach Trip Safety Flags

When you're vacationing at the beach, look out for colored flags that indicate whether it's safe to be in the water and what measures you'll need to take if you choose to enter. While the flags below are commonly used on US beaches, flags around the world will use a similar warning system; it's important to research what the caution flags mean in your particular location.

- **DOUBLE RED.** Water closed to the public
- **RED.** High hazard, with strong currents and/or high surf
- **YELLOW.** Medium hazard, with moderate surf and/or currents

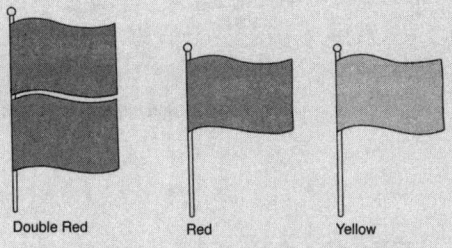

- **GREEN.** Low hazard, with calm conditions, but caution still advised
- **PURPLE.** Dangerous marine life, such as jellyfish or stingrays, present
- **RED/YELLOW (HALVED RED OVER YELLOW).** Area protected by lifeguards

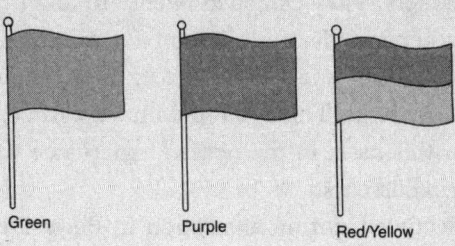

- **BLACK/WHITE (QUARTERED).** Designated area for non-powered watercraft, such as surfboards
- **YELLOW FLAG WITH CENTRAL BLACK BALL.** Surfboards and other non-powered watercraft prohibited
- **RED/WHITE (QUARTERED).** Emergency evacuation

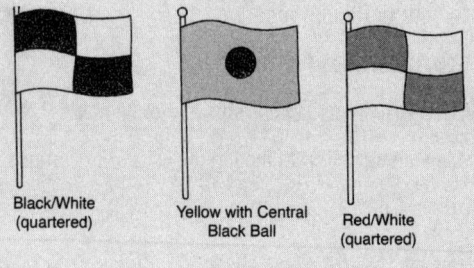

Source: United States Lifeguard Association

Surviving a Rip Current

A rip current is a powerful, fast-moving flow of water that pulls away from the shore. These currents typically form where waves break, creating a buildup of water that flows back out to sea through narrow channels, between sandbars, or underwater structures like piers. They can span twenty to one hundred feet in width and reach speeds of more than five miles per hour. Rip currents are dangerous and can be deadly, even when the waves aren't particularly large. This is a topic I have significant on-the-ground (or, in this case, in-the-ocean) experience with, having survived two rip currents.

The first occurred during a vacation in Playa Del Carmen, Mexico, when I was eight. My mom and I were standing on a sandbar when suddenly the tide shifted and we found ourselves in deep water. I vividly remember clinging to my mom in panic. She remained calm, treading water, and told me firmly, "You can't hold on to me. I need you to swim." With that, she swam behind me and pushed my feet forward as we moved parallel to clear the riptide, then diagonally toward the shore. Eventually we emerged three resorts down from where we'd first entered the water.

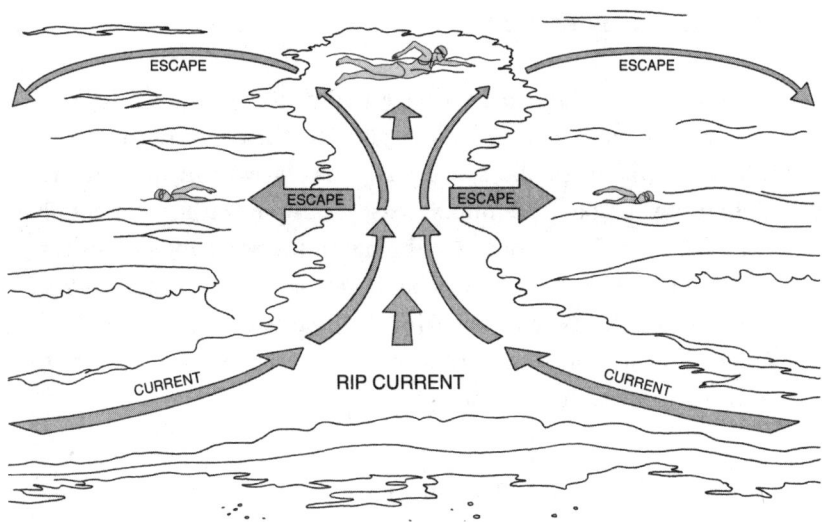

That moment was a wake-up call, and it sparked my dad to teach me how to handle rip currents, information that proved crucial years later when I found myself yet again being dragged out to sea. This time it was at our traditional post–soccer tournament beach gathering in San Diego—and I could hear my dad's advice echoing in my head: *Stay calm.*

If you ever find yourself caught in a rip current, the most important thing is to stay calm. Panic and hyperventilation can quickly drain your energy, leading to exhaustion and the risk of drowning. Instead, conserve your strength by floating or calmly treading water, and here's the kicker: Go with the flow. You have to let the rip current take you out to sea. Once it starts to dissipate, swim parallel to the shoreline until you're free from the current, and then swim at a diagonal back to land. Remember that where you exit the water could be quite a distance from where you entered. All that matters is that you *do* exit.

Street Harassment

While men are known to behave badly all over the world, residents of some regions have a reputation for being more overtly disrespectful in public spaces. If you're a woman, particularly when traveling to unfamiliar areas, it's important to be mentally prepared for the possibility of being on the receiving end of catcalling or other street harassment. Unfortunately, many women experience this type of behavior, and while no one should have to endure it, knowing how to respond can help you feel more confident in such situations.

If you're being catcalled in public . . .

- Ignore the catcaller. Walk with a clear sense of direction like you have somewhere to be and you know exactly where you're going. Don't address the person directly. It's usually safest not to engage.

- If the catcaller begins to follow you, stay in a well-populated area and keep as much distance as possible between you and them; don't let them get close to you, and if they do,

- bust out your personal key chain alarm, pepper gel, or whatever personal protection you have on you.
- If you don't have any personal protection, don't be afraid to ask for help: Look for a security guard, police officer, or shop manager. You can even walk up to a group of strangers, tell them that you're being followed, and ask if you can walk with them to get help.
- If you're unable to keep your distance and can't find anyone to help, scream, run, or fight (in no particular order). Make as much commotion as you can and do your best *never* to allow anyone to grab you and pull you away.

If you're being followed on foot in a store . . .

- Trust your intuition. If something feels off, there's a good chance it is.
- Stay in the most well-populated area you can and keep your distance from the person following you. Don't try to make a run for it or leave the store on your own.
- Be nonconfrontational but aware and assertive. Keep your head held high and walk with purpose. Make it known that you're not an easy target.
- If you're feeling scared, don't be afraid to tell a store employee what's going on or to ask a security guard or employee to walk you to your car.
- Noise and distance are your friends, even inside a store—if push comes to shove and you're in immediate danger, make as much commotion as possible (this is where a

personal key chain alarm comes in handy; see page 210). If necessary, you can use pepper gel to create distance between you and the person trailing you.

- Once you're in your car, lock the doors immediately and drive away. Don't hang out in the car texting or looking at your phone. Never be a sitting duck.

- As you start to drive, make sure you're not being followed.

- Keep your personal protection on you and within easy reach.

- If you're feeling profoundly unsafe, call 911. They will tell you exactly what to do.

What to Do if You're Being Robbed

If anyone ever attempts to rob you while you're out, always assume the individual is armed (whether or not you see a weapon), and try to discreetly call 911 if possible. (Make sure you comply with the robber's demands. Give them your phone, wallet, or jewelry—don't fight. Your life is more valuable than any item. Try to remember as many details as possible about what they looked like (height, weight, eye color, clothing, car, and so on) so you can turn that information over to law enforcement.

What to Do If You're Arrested or Detained Overseas

Hopefully you will never experience being detained while on an international trip, but if you should find yourself in this situation, be sure to follow these guidelines from the US Department of State:

- Before you go, make sure your passport is valid for at least six months beyond your travel return date and that you have, if needed, the appropriate visa.

- Research any travel advisories issued for your destination issued by the Department of State.

- Familiarize yourself with the laws of the country you'll be visiting. They'll be different from your own. Don't make any assumptions—for example, don't pack chewing gum if you're going to Singapore! Remember, you'll be held to the same laws as everyone else there; tourists don't get a free pass.

- If you're arrested, ask the local authorities to immediately alert the US consulate or embassy where you are (or, if you're able, reach out yourself). The consulate can help you find a lawyer, reach out to friends and family back home, familiarize you with the local justice system, and help you set up a trust to assist you in getting financial support from your friends and family if needed. Be aware that the embassy or consulate *cannot* get you out of jail.

Reflect on This

A Secret Service agent once taught me that I could use the reflection created by windows, car doors, mirrors, or any reflective surface to help with situational awareness. If you're passing by a car or a store window, look quickly to see if anyone is behind you. If you're in a store and you get the sense that someone is a little too close, use a mirror to confirm. You can also use your phone to pretend you're taking a selfie or hold up a makeup compact to look behind you.

Public Transport

Public transportation is an inexpensive and straightforward way to get around in cities across the world, but it's also a prime place where potential victims can be targeted for theft, assault, or worse. Here are some ways to stay safe:

- Always share your daily itinerary with your check-in person.
- Know where you're going before you get on the bus, train, ferry, or other transportation method.
- Try to pick a seat that provides a good vantage point to observe your surroundings and doesn't leave you blocked in.
- On a train, subway, or commuter rail, choose an occupied car—an empty car can leave you vulnerable. Stay with the crowd.
- Hold your belongings in your lap. The chances of recovering an item that is lost or stolen is slim to none.

- Don't wear flashy or expensive jewelry or designer bags on public transportation, as these might draw unwanted attention.

- Stay alert. Your phone can wait—and it's an easy target for theft.

Safety in Ubers, Taxis, and Private Transport Buses

Tons of people use Uber, Lyft, and other rideshare services to get around. They're prevalent in cities across the globe for a reason: They're incredibly convenient. Of course, taxis and private buses and vans are also common, especially when traveling to and from an airport. Before you hop into any type of shared vehicle with a stranger, plan ahead. Do your research beforehand so you know which services are legitimate. A travel agent can also arrange transportation for you before your trip; they'll generally also know which areas of town are considered safe for tourists. (See page 81 for more about rideshares.)

Lie to Survive—Always!

You're never traveling alone, you are not staying alone, and a male figure is *obviously* meeting you at your destination.

Campus Chronicles

Navigating College Life

College life is an exciting time, and if you're tackling that adventure now (or if you're already midway through it), I want you to enjoy every moment—while also staying safe. Although there's more awareness around campus safety today than there was, say, twenty years ago, no place is ever 100 percent safe, and colleges are no exception.

I went to school at the University of Nevada, Las Vegas for my freshman year, so my college experience wasn't particularly "normal," and the famous saying "what happens in Vegas stays in Vegas" doesn't necessarily apply when you're an adventurous young person! Our college parties often took place in hotel rooms and suites on the Vegas strip, not in a dorm or fraternity house. I remember feeling a little in over my head, like I was playing with the big dogs. One of the first parties I ever went to was in a well-known hotel—in a suite with stripper poles! Shortly after that, I remember walking into another party to see kids prepping a substance I didn't recognize. I turned to a stranger, and asked, "What's that?" They told me it was black-tar heroin, then asked, "You want in?"

"Oh, I'm good!" I said, then turned around and walked right back out, thinking, "What am I doing here?" In retrospect, I could have gotten myself into some very bad situations in Vegas, but my developing street smarts managed to keep me safe.

In recent years, colleges have increasingly prioritized safety through measures like enhanced on-campus programs, emergency communication methods, mental health resources, and more. Still, overall campus safety stats vary widely between schools and locations. While many colleges have made strides in improving their safety protocols, challenges like ever-evolving criminal activity and growing mental health issues mean it's always important to stay vigilant. Fortunately, you can take strategic actions to reduce your risk of being a target—and, as usual, it's important to live aware, not in fear. This chapter offers some strategies that can help keep you safe while away at college.

Remember the Red Zone

The red zone—the period of time between the start of the school year and Thanksgiving break—is statistically when you're most susceptible to sexual assault on campus. It's a time rife with parties and sporting events—an easy time to let your guard down, all while dealing with a new living environment, new friends and roommates, and fresh academic stressors. Incoming freshmen are especially vulnerable, as they haven't had time yet to develop their college-level street smarts.

To help offset the risks of the red zone, always do the following:

- Go out in groups.

- Establish a wing person—a trusted friend who always has your back in a social setting.

- Don't isolate yourself or let anyone isolate you from your group.
- Don't walk alone at night.
- Treat situational awareness as your first line of defense. Trust your gut, and switch locations if something or someone makes you feel uncomfortable.
- Always watch your drink and get a new one if it ever leaves your line of sight. If you're not feeling right and think you might have been drugged, tell a friend immediately—don't wander outside, leave the premises, or even go to the bathroom by yourself.
- Carry a form of easily accessible personal protection that you feel comfortable using and that is legal on campus (see page 207).

If You're the Fresh Meat on Campus . . .

Freshman year offers a wild mix of excitement and uncertainty. You're in a completely new environment, surrounded by people you don't know, trying to figure out whom to trust and how to navigate situations you've never been in before. The key to staying safe is learning to trust your instincts while also remembering that discomfort doesn't always equal danger. Feeling uneasy because something is unfamiliar is totally normal—your brain is adjusting to an all-new environment. With that said, you don't need a "good reason" to remove yourself from a place or situation that feels unsafe to you. You're always better off erring on the side of safety.

Friend groups as freshmen can be ever-changing; my friend group changed many times during my first semester alone.

You're going to get into a lot of casual conversations with all kinds of people, even just standing in line at the cafeteria. Any of these unfamiliar situations can be a path toward making a new friend—one of my best friends from college was someone I sat next to in my very first crim class. You just never know where a new friend will come from.

Even though most of the people you're meeting are students and it's a generally safe environment, you still don't know someone until you actually know them—so be friendly, but proceed with caution and always trust that little voice in the back of your head. Do what feels right for you when it comes to people you choose to let into your life as friends. But *do* make it a choice; it's easy to fall in with a convenient group of people, even if they're not the best fit.

Many freshmen are assigned a roommate at random, and this might be the first time you're sharing space with a stranger. But some colleges now let you request or choose your roommate yourself. If you're able to choose someone for yourself, don't just judge them by their social media; make sure to Facetime them and get a vibe check. It's important to have early conversations about boundaries and establish what will and won't work for you both when it comes to things like visitors. Make sure to discuss the days and times that you're both comfortable inviting people into the room (for example, you're not going to have people over when your roommate is prepping for a big test)—and after you're rooming together, make sure you talk about this regularly, as schedules are bound to change. Also, be sure to discuss respecting each other's valuables (laptops, important documents, and so on). It's a great idea for each of you to have your own safe. Last, have the safety precaution talk, which entails things like always locking your doors and windows (this is a must, no matter what), being mindful of whom you share your dorm room number and location with, and whom you bring home with you.

Safety 101

There's nothing complicated about staying safe on campus. It involves little more than learning what safety measures your school already has in place and implementing a few precautions of your own.

Familiarize Yourself with Your School's Escort System and Emergency Phones

Many colleges have an escort system set up that lets you request a security guard or student volunteer to safely accompany you home. Save the phone number for this service and use it if you're out and need a lift home for any reason. That's literally what these services are for!

Also, many colleges have emergency phones scattered around campus. They are typically lit with a blue light and have a red emergency button that you press to let campus security know you need help. Wherever you are on campus, know where the nearest emergency phone is—you or someone else might need it.

Practice Dorm Safety

- **TAKE A SAFETY WORKSHOP.** A lot of colleges offer self-defense classes or safety workshops. These can provide useful practical skills and knowledge about what to do if you find yourself in a crisis. The more prepared and aware you are, the better you'll be able to keep yourself safe. It's also a great way to meet safety-minded friends.

- **WATCH YOUR DORM ENTRANCES.** Never let a random person enter your dorm building behind you and never open the door to someone unless you're sure they live in the building. The doors lock automatically for a reason. If you feel like you're being followed, call 911 or campus security immediately and move to a well-lit, well-populated area.

Keep Your Phone Fully Charged and Use Location Sharing

This tip may seem obvious, but having a fully charged phone (and a backup way to charge it) is particularly important—it's literally your lifeline. It ensures that you can make emergency calls if you find yourself in a dangerous situation. Staying connected is also crucial for quickly reaching campus security or local authorities, using safety and map apps as you move around campus, and letting friends and family know where you are. Many colleges also have emergency notification systems that send out alerts about campus incidents, and a charged phone ensures that you'll receive these safety updates in real time. Bring a charged power bank with you if you're worried about your phone dying while you're out, and always keep a charging cord in your bag or purse.

It might seem extreme, but for safety's sake, it's best to have someone who knows where you are at any given time. Tell a roommate, tell a friend, tell your mom—just tell *someone* your plan for each day. Because plans can change, share your phone's location with trusted friends or family, so they can see if you're somewhere you didn't intend to be.

Be Savvy on Social Media: The College Edition

Social media is a fun way to connect with friends—just be sure your location is turned off, and be mindful about the people you add or follow. In a similar vein, don't tag your location on *any* social media stories or posts you make; keeping your whereabouts private makes it harder for you to be tracked or targeted. Make it a habit to get the green light before sharing your friends' photos on social media—and they should do the same for you.

Always Lock Your Doors and Windows

I'm always shocked by how common it is for college students to leave their doors and windows unlocked. Don't do this! College dorms can be vulnerable to theft, especially with students constantly on the go and so many visitors coming in and out. By simply locking your doors and windows, you protect yourself, your roommates, and your belongings while also maintaining your privacy. Making this small habit part of your routine significantly reduces the risk of break-ins and creates a safer environment—letting you enjoy college life with more peace of mind. Getting home from class? Lock the door. Heading down the hall to grab a snack from the vending machine? Lock the door. Getting in late after a night out with the girls? Lock the door. Lock, lock, lock!

Buy a Battery-Powered Doorstop Alarm

I have a few of these doorstop alarms, which I refuse to travel without (see page 130). They're also great for your dorm room door. This battery-powered alarm is incredibly simple to use. You place it right behind your door, and no one will be able to enter your room without an alarm blaring. It's so loud that it won't just wake you up, it'll wake up your neighbors too (and scare the hell out of the person trying to break into your room). This tool works best if you live alone or if you and your roommates are all home for the night.

Avoid Walking Alone, Especially at Night

It's always a good idea to walk with friends, whether day or night. This not only provides a layer of protection but also gives you a sense of security—there's strength in numbers! But sometimes walking alone is unavoidable. When you're walking around campus solo, especially at night, you'll need to be extra vigilant. Keep your head out of your cell phone. A distracted person is an easy target. Because theft, harassment, or assault are more likely to take place when you're alone, you'll want to always appear confident and alert and be aware of who and what is around you. Parts of campus may have insufficient lighting and less foot traffic, making you more vulnerable to crime.

Situational awareness is *everything*. One time in college, I was walking back to my car after a night class. I'd parked in a garage, and as I made my way to my car, I noticed a man wandering around who immediately seemed out of place. He was staring at me and moving in my direction. Instantly, my internal alarms went off. I knew I had two options—either run or come up with a lie to survive. Thinking fast, I looked toward a group of parked cars in the distance and called out, "John! Matt! Are we good for drinks?" The moment I did, the man stopped in his tracks. Without hesitation, he turned and headed down the stairwell. I sprinted to my car, jumped in, and locked the doors. My heart was beating out of my chest, but I had extricated myself from a potentially unsafe situation and that's all that mattered.

Being able to think on your feet and act confident can completely change the outcome of a situation. If you're taking a night class like I was, keep these safety tips in mind:

- Sign up with a friend or two, so you can travel to and from class in a group.

- Plan your route to class in advance, choosing the safest, most well-lit path. Use campus maps to familiarize yourself with the area.

- Check in with someone before you leave for class, letting them know where you're headed and when you expect to be back.

- Stay alert and aware of your surroundings. Avoid distractions and keep your personal protection device handy.

- If you're driving, park in a busy, well-lit area.

- Carry only what you need. Keep valuables like laptops and phones hidden and secure.

- Before leaving class, get your keys out so you're prepared when you approach your car.

- If something feels off, take a different route or seek help from campus security. Don't hesitate to call for an escort (some schools also offer shuttle buses).

Real-World Safety Story

> Back when I was in college, I used to travel home for weekends. When returning to my dorm, I always took the train—usually the last one, so I could have more time at home. This also meant I needed to walk from the train station to my room in the dark. I always took the path along the street, which was well lit and somewhat well populated with drivers. I also always talked on the phone as I walked, so someone knew I was okay.

One night I noticed a person behind me and something immediately felt off. I held my pepper spray inside my jacket pocket and kept walking back to campus at a normal pace. He followed. The last bit of my way home was almost completely unlit, but it was the only way home, so I had to take it. That's when he walked faster and came closer. The guy I was speaking with on the phone was in another city, but I loudly told him that I was almost there and asked if he could step out and help me with my suitcase.

I was lucky that some other student was standing and smoking at the front door of the dorm when I arrived. As soon as my pursuer saw the guy, he turned and left, no doubt assuming he was my friend on the phone.

—Steffi

THE TAKEAWAY

Always stay aware of your surroundings and don't hesitate to lie to survive.

At the Campus Gym or Laundry Facility

If you're in a space you need a key to access, like a gym, laundry facility, outdoor patio, or roof deck, never open the door to someone you don't know. I know it's awkward to ignore someone knocking, but in the world we live in, letting a stranger in is not a risk you should be willing to take. Err on the side of caution and don't open that door. If the person lives there, they should have a key. Sure, it's possible they simply forgot their key, but it's also possible that it's a person with ill intentions.

Script It Out

SOMEONE WANTS INTO YOUR SPACE

If a stranger tries to gain entrance to a shared space like a laundry room or gym while you're inside, avoid engaging with them. Pretend not to notice them or act like you're on the phone. If they persist and don't leave, trust your instincts—call campus police or security, let them know where you are, and explain that someone is trying to get in and you don't feel comfortable. You could also call a trusted (male) friend to come by and assist. If avoiding conversation isn't possible, firmly but politely say something like "I'm sorry, I can't let you in. I've had a bad experience before, and campus security is already on the way." Prioritize your safety over being polite.

Going-Out Guidelines

- **BE SMART WITH DRUGS.** It's more important now than ever to be smart when it comes to experimenting with drugs. It's impossible to know what street drugs can be laced with, and fentanyl (a dangerous and highly lethal opioid) is everywhere. It's always best to err on the side of caution—a simple "no, thanks" could save your life.

- **KNOW YOUR RISKS.** Educate yourself and your friends on what might be floating around campus. A perfect example: As of this writing, pink cocaine (aka Tusi) is a dangerous mix of street drugs that's been dyed pink and mixed into a powder form. The concoction often includes little to no cocaine and is instead a mishmash of drugs like MDMA, caffeine, ketamine, opioids, methamphetamines, and other psychoactive substances. It's popular among teens and young adults who are out partying, and side effects include nausea, hallucinations, rapid heartbeat, seizures, respiratory issues, and even death. Next year there will be another scary combination out there. Moral of the story: You never truly know what ingredients you're ingesting, so it's always best to take a pass.

> **CLOUDED JUDGMENT.** As your level of alcohol intake increases, the quality of your decision-making decreases. Never climb on roofs, hang off balconies, or swim in unknown ponds or lakes. And NEVER dive headfirst into unfamiliar bodies of water. In fact, it's safest to avoid swimming altogether when you're intoxicated.

Staying Safe at Parties

- Don't drink the Kool-Aid—literally! Don't drink concoctions like "jungle juice" or punch—or anything at all unless you know exactly what's in it and where it came from.

- Never isolate yourself in a random room with a stranger(s). Parties are loud, and if you run into trouble and need to yell for help, there's a chance that no one will hear you.

- Stay with your friends—there's safety in numbers.

- Never drive drunk or otherwise compromised. Call an Uber or ask a friend to pick you up.

Have a Sober Buddy

When I was in college, my friends and I would take turns being the sober one on our nights out (though I have to admit, I was usually the designated sober friend—I guess some things never change). If you're going out drinking with a group, consider doing the same—take turns appointing someone as the sober (or mostly sober) point person. This friend can help coordinate transportation, keep an eye on everyone, and stay sharp in case anything unexpected happens. It's a simple way to ensure your group has fun while knowing someone always has your back.

The Rules on Ridesharing

For female college students, it's crucial to stay cautious when using Uber or other ridesharing apps, especially after a night out (for more on this, see page 81). Always double-check the details on your app—compare the car's make, model, and license plate with the description on your app, and verify the driver's name and photo before getting in. Once you're in the car, stay alert. Don't get distracted by your phone, and keep an eye on your surroundings to ensure the route you're on is correct. If your driver takes an unusual detour and can't explain why, trust your instincts. If you can safely exit at the next opportunity, get out and run.

If I were in that situation, I'd first ask the driver where he was headed or what route he's taking, pointing out that we're going the wrong direction. If he refused to answer, I'd check to see if the doors are unlocked. If they were, as stated above, I'd exit at the next stop sign or stoplight. If the doors and windows were locked, meaning child locks were engaged, that's a red flag for my safety. In this case, I'd tell the driver I wasn't feeling well and needed to get out (remember: lie to survive). If he still refused, I'd take action: This is when personal protection becomes essential. I always carry pepper gel and a compact window-breaking tool on my key chain, and if necessary, I'd use them to escape (see page 207 for more on

> personal safety tools). Other options could be a stun gun or tactical pen (note: while both of these items are effective, for me they are a last resort because you don't want to get into a situation where you could be overpowered and your weapons are used against you).
>
> While these might seem extreme, it's important to know your options and have layers of protection. Bottom line: I'm not waiting around to find out where I'm headed if a driver refuses to explain why they're taking me in the wrong direction.

Mental Health Check

Living aware means more than just being perceptive about what other people are doing. Your personal safety starts with your awareness of how you're feeling internally. You're the only person who truly knows what's going on inside your head—no one else knows you like you do.

Mental health struggles are increasingly affecting teens and young adults, and it's a topic we need to address openly and with compassion. While college is supposed to be a time for exploring and learning about who you are and what you want from life, it can also be a roller coaster of overwhelm, stress, and anxiety. According to the National Library of Medicine, suicide is the second-leading cause of death for college students.[*] Many college campuses are implementing resources designed specifically for suicide prevention. If you or someone you know is struggling

---

[*] Yunyu Xiao et al., "Suicide Prevention Among College Students Before and During the COVID-19 Pandemic: Protocol for a Systematic Review and Meta-analysis," *JMIR research protocols* vol. 10,5 e26948, https://doi.org/10.2196/26948.

with thoughts of suicide, please understand that there is absolutely no shame in reaching out for help. You are not alone, and you don't have to navigate this pain by yourself.

It's important to have a support system so you don't internalize your struggles on your own. The Suicide and Crisis Lifeline is available 24/7 in the United States—simply text or call 988.

Stay Cyber-Smart

Protecting Yourself in the Digital Jungle

Technology is advancing at a breakneck pace, and it feels like every day there's a new development (or fifty). While this has many benefits, the online universe has its dangers; from AI fraud risks to online scams to phishing emails, it's never been more important to stay vigilant when it comes to your online safety.

I've been the target of plenty of online scams—phishing texts, emails, you name it. But one of the most recent attempts was so obvious that I spotted it from a mile away. One day, my management team forwarded me an email that seemed a little too good to be true. It claimed that a well-known celebrity's podcast wanted to feature me but with one catch—it had to be a livestream hosted through my social media accounts. They offered an eye-popping amount of money, which was my first red flag. Then the email reassured me: "Don't worry, we'll send you all the links and instructions you'll need to access your account prior to the event."

I'm still not sure what the ultimate goal was—maybe to hijack my social media account for ransom—but I wasn't about to find out. When something feels off, it's always better to be safe than sorry. I immediately flagged the email to my management team, and needless to say, we politely declined this so-called opportunity.

By staying on top of dangerous trends and honing your instincts, you can significantly reduce your risk of falling victim to internet scams, identity theft, and other types of trouble.

Be Mindful of Your Digital Footprint

Keep in mind that anything you post online can stick around forever. Even if you delete something, there's a solid chance it's already been saved, shared, or archived. The internet never forgets, and once something is out there, it can be impossible to completely erase, so it's always a smart idea to think twice before sending or posting.

You already know what I think about sharing personal information, whether it's photos, your location, or even just your thoughts: Always be cautious. It's not just about who you're sharing it with right now but also about what could happen in the future. People change, relationships end, and things you thought were private can come back to haunt you. Sexually charged photos or messages are especially risky. Even if you're comfortable sending them to someone you trust, there's always the possibility they could be leaked or shared without your permission, and once they're out there, it's incredibly hard to get them back. If someone is asking you to share information or images and your instincts tell you to be wary, ask yourself, "Why does this person want me to send this?" and "What's the worst that could happen?"

Just the Facts

> In 2023, almost 18,000 Americans were the victims of online romance scams (more on these scams on page 165), losing about $650 million in total.*

Have Super-Strong Passwords

This may seem basic, but having strong passwords is essential for protecting your online accounts from unauthorized access. As tempting as it may be, you should *never* use "password" as your password (yep, lots of people still do this!). Weak passwords like this are among the first things hackers try when attempting to break into an account.

To create a hard-to-guess password, use a variety of characters that make it much more difficult for anyone (including automated hacking tools) to crack. Start by including a mix of uppercase and lowercase letters, as this increases the password's complexity. Incorporating numbers and special characters like @, $,! or * further strengthens your password, making it harder to guess. Also avoid using easily guessed information, such as your name, birthdate, or a pet's name. Your password should be something that isn't obvious, even to people who might know you well, and a longer password (ideally twelve or more characters) can make it significantly harder for a hacker to break into your account.

---

* "Don't Let a Romance Scammer Steal Your Heart and Savings," *FBI Sacramento Press Office*, February 13, 2025, https://www.fbi.gov/contact-us/field-offices/sacramento/news/-dont-let-a-romance-scammer-steal-your-heart-and-savings.

Create a strong new password for each account; avoid reusing passwords across multiple sites or services. If you're worried about remembering all your complex passwords, consider using a password manager to securely store and generate your passwords. Also, remember that the longer your password is, the better. Stay proactive and update your passwords regularly to further safeguard your digital security.

Create Separate Email Accounts for Separate Purposes

I have one personal email for communication with friends and family, another for any work-related matters, and yet another dedicated solely to online shopping and nonessential sign-ups. This helps keep my important accounts secure while also reducing spam. The email I use for shopping is unrelated to my real name, social media, or banking accounts, which adds an extra layer of privacy.

I also use an alias when shopping online or having packages delivered to my house. This hasn't caused a problem for me as far as package delivery goes, and this extra step helps protect my identity and keeps my personal details more secure, especially in case of a data breach or package mix-up.

By keeping separate emails and using an alias, I can hold more control over my personal information.

Determine if an Email or Text Is Legitimate

Scammers often use addresses that look close to the real thing, but with minor changes, like extra letters or numbers. So the first step in deciding if an email is legit is to carefully check the sender's email address or phone number. If you notice a message from "support@amazonn.com" instead of "support@amazon.com," that's an obvious red flag.

Now look at the body of the email or the text message itself. If it feels super urgent, too good to be true, or contains grammatical or spelling errors, chances are it's a scam. Legitimate companies don't send random messages asking for money (or your personal info).

Think Before You Click Links in Texts or Emails

Random links in texts and emails could be part of a phishing scam. If there's a link in the message, hover over it, without clicking, to reveal the URL. If it doesn't match the official site or looks fishy, skip it. Cybercriminals often use these links to trick you into giving out personal information like passwords or credit card details. The links might look legit at first, but they can lead to fake websites designed to steal your data or infect your device with malware. Even if the email or text seems like it came from a reliable source, hackers can easily spoof phone numbers or email addresses to make their messages seem real. If you're not sure whether a link is legit, call or email the company the message came from and ask them directly. But always pause before clicking, no matter how urgent the message seems. The urgency is built in as part of the scam!

Also, opening attachments, especially from people you don't know, is risky—they could be carrying viruses or malware. These can infect your computer or phone, steal your personal information, or give hackers access to your personal accounts. Scammers are really good at making attachments look like harmless photos or documents, so it's easy to get tricked.

If you get an email you weren't expecting that comes with an attachment, don't open it right away; try texting or calling the person to double-check if they actually sent it. And if you're still unsure, it's a good idea to delete the email or scan the file with antivirus software before opening it. Better safe than sorry.

Be Wary of Websites You've Never Heard Of

Don't give your personal details—name, email, phone number, and so on—to websites you've never heard of. There's simply no way to tell what these sites will do with your information. Here are a few of the hazards:

- **SCAMS AND FRAUD.** Some websites are set up specifically to deceive users, and they're offering fake products or services. These could potentially steal your payment info.

- **MALWARE AND VIRUSES.** Unfamiliar websites are more likely to host malware, which can corrupt your device, steal your personal info, or compromise your security.

- **DATA HARVESTING.** Some sites collect personal data without appropriate disclosures, which puts your privacy at risk. They could also sell your information to third parties without your consent.

To stay safe online, make sure the site you're on is legitimate. Does it have clear, verifiable contact info? Is everything spelled correctly? Also check your browser address bar and make sure it has "https" in the browser (a lock symbol should show too).

A Few of the Most Common Online Scams

- **ROMANCE OR DATING SCAMS.** These scams occur when someone lies about their identity or pretends to be someone else in order to lure a target into a romantic "relationship." After the target is sucked in, the scammer asks for money, gift cards, or other forms of payment. Some scammers will pretend they're in the middle of a critical emergency and in need of immediate funds. Others may go so far as proposing marriage and promising to meet up one-on-one. Romance scams can happen to anyone, though older adults are the most common victims. How to know if you're being scammed? Use Google's reverse image search to see if the photos of the person you're talking to match up with anyone else online. Watch out for love-bombing and overly intense or passionate language early in the "relationship." Also, be wary if the person seems evasive and noncommittal in their answers to your questions. They might ask you to move the conversation offline or to a less secure mode of communication, and they will at some point ask for money. If you believe you're being scammed, stop communicating with the person right away. Check your bank accounts and other financial accounts to be sure no funds have been stolen. Then report the incident to the Federal Trade Commission and the police, if necessary. You can also file a complaint with the FBI's Internet Crime Complaint Center.

- **PHISHING.** Phishing attempts are usually emails and texts sent by scammers with the intention of "fishing" for your personal info, like your log-in credentials, bank account number, password, or credit card number. They're commonly disguised as "real" emails from companies you know and trust, like your bank, Netflix, or Google. They often have a sense of urgency, lack a personalized greeting, contain typos or errors, and ask for some sort of sensitive information from you.

A phishing email might:

- Say there's a problem with your account or payment details
- Warn of suspicious activity or unauthorized log-in attempts on your account
- Include a fraudulent invoice
- Ask you to click a link to make a payment
- Request that you confirm or update your personal information
- Claim you qualify for a government refund

What to do if you suspect you're the target of a phishing attack? Don't reply to the text message or email; don't share any personal info; and do a Google search for the text from the message to see if others have gotten the same one. Report it if possible, delete it, and move on with your day.

❱ **LOTTERY OR SWEEPSTAKES SCAMS.** In a lottery scam, the perpetrators deceive you into believing you've won a large prize in a fake contest. Often, they will request money or personal information, telling you this is required for you to claim your prize. In a lottery scam, they'll ask for a certain amount of money in order to release your complete winnings. They may refer to this as a customs fee, tax, shipping or service charge, or an unspecified "withholding." In many cases, they will instruct you to pay this fee through a wire transfer or a money transfer service like Western Union. Again, you'll notice a sense of urgency in the communication from these scammers, insisting that you must act right away if you want to claim your prize. This is not the way a real lottery or sweepstakes is run. Also, watch out for vague or generic details in the message you receive; for instance, the letter might address you as "sir or madam" instead of using your full name. If you get an email, phone call, or any other type of communication claiming you've won a lottery or a sweepstakes for a contest you never entered, don't fall for it—and definitely don't respond to the scammers' requests.

But Wait! There's More!

Here are a few other scams to watch out for. In every case, do not respond.

- **SCAM TEXTS PRETENDING TO BE BANKS.** With this scam, watch out for a text or call from your "bank" asking if you approved a large transaction.

- **FAKE JOB OFFERS.** If you get a random message from a stranger offering a job that sounds like easy money—it's usually from a scammer. Ignore it.

- **"FREE GIFT" MESSAGES.** Do not respond to texts or emails purported to be from large retailers claiming you've won a free gift or prize, even a small one. If you click the link and enter the shipping fee, you'll turn over your credit card info to the scammer.

- **FAKE PACKAGE DELIVERY.** You might get a text pretending to be from the USPS or UPS, claiming that there are issues delivering a package to your address and asking you to update your information online.

- **TECH SUPPORT SCAMS.** In these scams, you'll receive a call or email from someone claiming to be from a tech support service offering to help you with your computer. Their aim is to access the contents of your computer and steal information.

- **CHARITY SCAMS.** Someone claiming to be affiliated with a charity (either real or fictitious) may call or email you asking for a donation. This is especially common after a big disaster. Verify that the charity exists and that the person is part of said charity before giving (but better yet, give when not under pressure—and always through a trusted charity website).

Safe Banking

If you get a call from a number claiming to be your bank, don't pick it up. If you *do* pick up, don't give out any personal information on the call, no matter what the person asks you. In fact, never give out *any* personal information on an inbound call that claims to be from a financial institution. If you have doubts about whether the call is legit, hang up the phone immediately. Banks will never ask you to share your pin or your password. They won't text you asking you to verify your account number or ask you to share any kind of code with them. Sign in to your bank accounts only from the bank's website or app, never through a text or email. And if you have any concerns about whether you may have been scammed by someone claiming to be from your bank, simply walk into your closest bank branch and ask to talk to someone about it. They can evaluate your accounts with you and determine what's going on.

Artificial Intelligence and Internet Fraud

AI is the current talk of the tech universe, and every day it's being used in new ways for a variety of applications (both helpful and bizarre). But when it comes to AI and internet fraud, there's a lot to watch out for.

- **ROMANCE SCAMS.** As mentioned, romance scams are on the rise—and AI makes it easier to fool people than ever before. A new wave of romance scammers is using AI to create false audio, photos, and videos. It's literally possible to create a fake online "human," and the technological advancements around AI make it extremely difficult to tell an AI person from a real one.

- **VOICE CLONING.** In this scenario, scammers take a brief audio clip of someone's voice, then use AI to create a convincing bogus recording of the person claiming to be in desperate trouble and in need of money. For instance, a scammer could use AI to replicate your friend's voice. Then you get a call from said "friend"—from their real phone number—claiming to have been kidnapped and in need of ransom money to escape the perpetrators.

- **DEEP FAKES.** Scammers can use AI to create realistic-looking fake photos of celebrities, public figures, or even your regular friends and family. These photos can be used in appeals for donations or other requests for monetary help.

- **PHISHING.** Generative AI (like ChatGPT) can help scammers draft legitimate-sounding emails without grammatical or other errors, making their targets more likely to click on them. These emails are convincing and appear to be from your bank, mortgage lender, shopping site, or other prominent website.

One way to help offset these AI-fueled scam risks is to come up with a family code word that only members of your immediate family know; this way, if you get any strange family-related email requests or phone calls, you can ask for the code word before continuing to engage.

If You're the Victim of Revenge Porn or Online Sextortion

Sextortion can happen to anyone, whether you're fourteen or sixty-five—but teens are frequently targeted. Online sextortion is essentially blackmail: threatening to release sexual images or videos of the victim unless they cough up money or provide additional sexually driven images or videos. Young people are frequent targets of this type of sextortion through social media or online gaming, and often the perpetrator will offer up a sexual image first (this is usually either AI-generated or an actual photo of someone who appears their age). The target is then convinced to share an image of their own or participate in a sexually motivated livestream where the perpetrator can screen-record or save images. The perp may increase their demands depending on what they're receiving back from the target. They may threaten to release the images to the victim's friends, family, social media accounts, or classmates.

Revenge porn is a type of nonconsensual pornography in which sexual photos or videos of the victim are released without their consent, often by a partner or former partner. Sometimes this is done as a vindictive act, and sometimes it's done simply because the perpetrator feels like it. No matter the motive, it's never okay (it's also illegal in almost every state).

So what should you do if you're a target of revenge porn or another kind of sextortion?

- Screenshot all the messages you've received thus far; document everything, including any nonconsensually released images or posts. It may be uncomfortable to document these things, but having a trail of evidence is important if you decide to report it to the authorities.
- Immediately stop messaging with the perpetrator. Block them on all platforms.
- Do not give in to any threats, either direct or implied, and *never* give the person money or any additional images that they're asking for. You might be able to stop a payment you've already sent if the funds were not yet collected.
- Report the content if it's already been released. Most social media platforms and websites take revenge porn seriously. Report the leaked images or videos directly on the platform—many have policies for removing nonconsensual content.
- Report the incident to the police. As noted above, revenge porn is illegal in most US states, so it's worth reaching out to your local authorities. They'll guide you on the next steps, so you don't have to go through it alone.
- Consider getting legal help. Lawyers who specialize in privacy or internet law can assist. They will know strategies to get content taken down and can also offer advice on protecting your rights and potentially pressing charges.
- Take care of yourself. This type of situation is incredibly emotionally challenging, so lean on friends, family, and/or a therapist. Having support can make an enormous difference.

Turn Off Location Services on Your Photos

Your location will automatically show up on your phone's photos unless you disable location services on them. Turning off the location feature on your photos prevents your exact whereabouts from being embedded in the image's metadata, or EXIF data. When you take a photo with location services enabled, your phone tags the photo with information about where it was taken (like GPS coordinates). This means anyone who views or shares the photo could potentially see where you've been (or where you are if you're posting in real time). If you're sharing photos with friends, or on social media, this could reveal personal details like your home address or other places you visit regularly. By disabling location on your photos, you reduce the chances of someone tracking your movements.

Turning off these services is simple; it should fall under your phone's settings, depending on what type of phone you have. A quick Google search can help you figure out how to disable the feature on your particular model.

The Safe Side of Social Media

As mentioned previously, when it comes to your social media activity, less is always more. Remember . . .

- Never post in real time, don't share your location on your photos, don't tag your location in real time, and be mindful of what's in the background of your images, especially if it reveals where you live, work, or go to school. Look for street names and names on buildings in particular.

- Don't share images and other information about your vacation until after the fact—no one needs to know when you're out of town and your home is vacant! It's a security risk for break-ins.

- To share things a bit more freely with a dedicated few people you trust, you can use the "close friends" Instagram story setting instead of blasting it out in public, but be selective.
- Another way to boost your online safety is to use a nickname on social media instead of using your full first and last name (I do this myself!).
- Don't put your town, city, or neighborhood in your bio. If you want to reference your location, keep it vague, such as "Northeast" or "West Coast vibes."
- Every social media app has settings for different security measures; be knowledgeable about what you're able to control and take as many security measures as possible to keep yourself safe.
- If you have kids, I suggest being incredibly cautious about posting pics of them online—I personally will never share mine. It's up to you, of course, but the data have shown that adult men make up a large portion of followers on accounts of young kids. If you do post photos of your child, be careful about what they're wearing; never show a uniform or anything that might reveal where they go to school or where they live.

Using Google to Your Advantage

❱ **DISABLE FACE RECOGNITION ON GOOGLE PHOTOS.** Disabling this feature helps safeguard your privacy and reduces the risk of your personal data being exploited. (The good news: If you're reading this book, you're probably one of the good guys.)

- **PROTECT YOUR PRIVACY.** Face recognition can be used to track and identify you without your permission. By turning it off, you'll ensure that your face isn't automatically tagged or linked to your identity in photos and videos, especially if they get shared without you knowing.

- **KEEP YOUR DATA SAFE.** Platforms store a ton of personal info, including your facial data. If this data gets hacked or misused, it could be a problem, especially if the platform's security isn't up to par. Disabling facial recognition gives you more control over your personal info, so you don't have to worry about it being used in ways you didn't agree to.

- **AVOID BEING WATCHED.** Having face recognition turned on makes it easier for people to track you, both online and in real life. And if your location is tagged, it makes it even simpler for others to follow your movements (a good reason why your location should never be enabled!).

- **LIMIT THIRD-PARTY ACCESS.** Turning off face recognition lowers the chance that advertisers or even law enforcement will be able to use your facial data for things like targeted ads or profiling without your consent.

❱ **SET UP GOOGLE ALERTS FOR YOUR NAME AND SOCIAL MEDIA HANDLES.** Set up a Google Alert for your name—it's a small but effective way to keep track of your digital footprint. The alert will notify you every time your name is mentioned online. Setting up an alert is an easy way to stay aware of what's being said about you on the internet, and it gives you a heads-up about potential privacy concerns or scams. You'll know exactly where your personal information is being shared, whether it's on social media, blogs, news sites, or online forums like Reddit. If confidential data like your contact info, address, or phone number appears somewhere unexpected or potentially harmful, a Google Alert will let you know right away, allowing you to take action quickly. And if someone is using your name to create fake accounts or post misleading information, you'll know, allowing you to address any identity theft before it spirals.

To set up a Google Alert, simply visit google.com/alerts and enter your name. You can also create as many alerts as you'd like for other family members (or simply for topics of interest to you). If you have a common name, try narrowing it down by adding specific details like your location or job title.

❱ **ADJUST GOOGLE MAPS' PRIVACY SETTINGS TO BLUR YOUR HOME IN STREET VIEW.** Blurring your home on Google Street View is a smart move for a few reasons. First off, it helps protect your privacy. When your house is easily visible online, anyone can scope out where you live. Blurring it makes it harder for strangers to pinpoint your exact location and generally gives you more control over who knows where you reside. It also helps protect you from potential crime since publicly available images of your house make it easier for burglars or scammers to target you. They might figure out when you're not home or gather other details that could put you at risk. Blurring your house simply means there's less information out there about you, which is never a bad thing.

To do it, go to maps.google.com, search for your home address, and click on the photo of your home when it appears, then click Report a Problem on the bottom-right of the screen. Next, use your mouse to tweak the view of the image so that your home (and anything else you want to blur out) is contained inside the red and black box. After this, you'll be asked what you're choosing to blur—simply click "my home." Then enter your email address and click "submit." Voilà!

> ### Avoid "Fun" Online Quizzes
>
> Don't fill out those silly online quizzes that ask you for things like the name of your first pet, the make and model of your first car, or the street you grew up on. The answers to these questions are all commonly used terms that people use to recover passwords. Revealing this info on a random quiz could inadvertently make your accounts easier to hack.

Layers of Defense

> **ALWAYS ENABLE MULTIFACTOR AUTHENTICATION (MFA).** Turning on multifactor authentication (MFA), also known as two-step verification, is one of the easiest ways to add an extra layer of security in keeping your online accounts safe. MFA is a security method that requires you to provide more than one form of identification to log in to an account. Instead of just using a password (which can be guessed or stolen), MFA requires an additional step to confirm it's really you. This could be a code sent to your phone; it could also be a fingerprint or facial recognition. So even if someone got ahold of your password, they still wouldn't be able to easily access your account. MFA is a second line of defense.
>
> MFA also helps prevent account takeovers, which are becoming more common. If someone gains access to your account, they could lock you out, change your password, and

start tampering with your data. But with MFA, that's less likely to happen since they'd need more than just your password to take control of the account. They will be going after lower-hanging fruit.

Most services, like Google, Facebook, and your bank, offer simple ways to enable MFA, whether it's through an app, a text message, your face or your fingerprint. It usually only takes a minute to set up. Make sure to indicate that you want to enable MFA anytime you're asked about it online.

- **ENABLE ALERTS FOR SUSPICIOUS LOG-INS.** On all your major accounts—including your bank accounts, Google, Facebook, your email account, and so on—it's crucial to enable alerts for any suspicious attempted log-ins. Enabling these alerts is important because it helps you detect unauthorized access early. The notifications will let you know if someone tries to log in from an unfamiliar location or device, which allows you to secure your account before anything goes south.

These alerts can help prevent identity theft, financial losses, and the release of sensitive personal info. They also give you a chance to act quickly if someone tries to take over your account or lock you out completely. When there is any unusual activity on your account, like, say, someone attempts to guess your password and break into your account, you'll receive a message from the website in question alerting you to that fact.

To enable these notifications, go to your account settings on the platform you want to monitor for suspicious log-ins. Look for a section related to security or privacy and choose the option to receive alerts about unusual log-in attempts. You should do this wherever possible so you can stay on top of what's going on in your most important and frequently used accounts.

❯ **AVOID PUBLIC CHARGING STATIONS.** Use your own charger for your electronics when you're traveling or on the go. Though they might seem convenient, those airport charging stations carry hidden risks, including:

- **JUICE JACKING.** This is when a public USB charging port is tampered with to steal your data. USB ports can carry both power *and* data, so when you plug your phone in, hackers could potentially access your personal info or even infect your phone with malware.

- **COMPROMISED DEVICES.** Even if the charging station appears safe and "normal-looking," someone could have messed with it or swapped out cables.

- **LACK OF ENCRYPTION.** Many charging stations don't have any security to protect your data while you're charging. That means if someone gets their hands on the port, they could potentially snoop on your phone or steal sensitive info like passwords or emails.

- **TOO MANY USERS.** These stations are used by lots of people, so the risks for everyone get heightened. Someone with bad intentions could take advantage of the opportunity to tamper with the entire system—or your device.

- **CARRY A POWER BANK.** The ideal option is to bring your own charger or portable power bank with you, so you don't need to rely on public stations.

- **USE A CHARGING-ONLY CABLE.** Some cables are designed exclusively for charging—no data transfer means no risk of hackers. If you plan on using a public charging station, get a charging-only cable.

- **USE A USB DATA BLOCKER.** These little gadgets let you charge your phone while blocking any data transfer, adding an extra layer of protection.

- **STICK TO WALL OUTLETS.** If you can, find a regular old AC outlet to plug your charger into. They don't carry data, so they're much safer.

Protect Your Data with RFID Blocking

For when you're on vacation or simply out and about, consider buying a purse or wallet that blocks radio frequency identification (RFID). RFID technology uses radio signals to retrieve data from an electronic chip embedded in an object. These chips, known as RFID tags, can transmit information from distances ranging from a few inches to several feet. RFID-blocking purses and wallets can help protect you from people using RFID-skimming tools to steal your credit card info—a scam in which a thief steals the card number from your chip-embedded card while walking past you. If this occurs, the person has to be super close to you—if you're in a public place and someone is standing or walking close beside your bag or purse, be careful. This is yet another reason to constantly practice situational awareness.

Mass Violence

What to Do When the Unthinkable Happens

It's tragic that I even have to include a chapter like this in a book about general day-to-day safety. In an ideal world, we wouldn't have to think about the possibility of a stranger with a gun walking into a classroom, a nightclub, a concert, or a parade and senselessly taking innocent lives. But unfortunately this *is* the world we live in.

A mass shooting is an act of targeted violence in which one or more perpetrators open fire in a public, often densely populated space with the intention of killing as many people as possible. Think about the devastation that unfolded on the Las Vegas Strip in 2017, or the Orlando nightclub massacre in 2016, or the tragedy at Sandy Hook Elementary in 2012. These incidents are unfathomable, yet this type of violence has been increasing since the COVID-19 pandemic in 2020. In fact, 2020 saw America's firearm homicide rate hit its highest level since 1994.*

---

* "*Vital Signs*: Changes in Firearm Homicide and Suicide Rates — United States, 2019 –2020," *CDC Morbidity and Mortality Weekly Report*, May 13, 2022, https://www.cdc.gov/mmwr/volumes/71/wr/mm7119e1.htm.

You often hear about these horrific tragedies on the news, and the response is always the same: "Thoughts and prayers." Each time it happens, you think, "This has to be it, things will change," but then another tragedy strikes just a week later. When you witness these events repeatedly, they start to feel like a grim social norm in the United States, but you never fully grasp the gravity of it until it impacts your own community. As mentioned in the introduction, that's what happened to me during the Highland Park Fourth of July parade shooting that left seven dead and more than forty injured. I never imagined I'd be able to say a mass shooting happened in *my* hometown, affecting people I know and love, but it's a harsh reminder that these things can happen anywhere, anytime, no matter how "safe" your community feels.

As I was writing this book, I was faced with yet another real-life reminder that danger can strike when you least expect it, and that mass violence doesn't discriminate. Days before I was due to submit this manuscript for my second round of editing, my cousin and I were in South Florida, enjoying a normal beach day—until suddenly it wasn't. Out of nowhere, we found ourselves in a massive crowd where instantly, I felt it—that deep, instinctual sense that something was wrong. My cousin felt it too. I looked at her and said, "We need to cross the street. Now." There was no hesitation. Just action. But that feeling didn't go away. As we briskly left the area, my heart was pounding, and I turned to my cousin again, saying, "I swear, I'm expecting to hear pop, pop, pop" (meaning gunfire). I didn't know why I felt that way; I just did. And I said it more than once. Less than an hour later, reports came out confirming that gunshots had been fired in that exact area. Another chilling reminder to always trust your gut, even when it doesn't fully make sense. Because that feeling? That instinct? It's there for a reason . . . and sometimes the only warning you'll get is the subtle one that can save your life.

The truth is, most of us have no idea what we'd do if we found ourselves in a mass violence incident. Would we flee? Try to hide? Fight back? What's the right move when your life is in imminent danger and everything is happening so quickly?

In this chapter, I'll lay out the best advice I can for these terrifying scenarios. I hope you'll never need to use this information, but being prepared is the first step toward keeping yourself safe in an unpredictable world.

> **NOTE:** *While this chapter focuses primarily on active shooters, not all mass-casualty incidents involve firearms. This advice also applies if an attacker is armed with knives, machetes, or other sorts of weapons. Also, remember that each mass violence situation is unique and unpredictable. The following tips should help you think on your feet and form a strategy, but they will not necessarily pertain to every instance of mass violence. If law enforcement is present and giving instructions, follow them immediately.*

Warning Signs

There are often red flags before school shootings or other mass violence incidents. Signs a potential perpetrator is reaching a breaking point include:

- Social withdrawal or isolation from family and friends
- Outright or obvious threats of violence

- Bringing up previous mass shootings or other incidents of violence
- Cruelty to animals
- Collecting weapons
- Violent outbursts
- Social media posts that allude to mass violence
- Expression of severe frustration with a school, institution, person, or group of people
- Verbalizing threats, such as "I'll shoot this place up" or "You're all going to be very sorry"

If you see or hear something, say something. Report threats to law enforcement; don't assume someone else will.

The Ten-Second Rule

Remember, situational awareness is paramount. As discussed in chapter 5, make it routine that anytime you enter a place, the first thing you do is take ten seconds to scan the area and familiarize yourself with the space. Look for all the exits; check out the location and size of the windows. Look at the people around you—do you notice anyone who appears off or is acting in an unusual manner? Practicing situational awareness can save your life, so don't skimp on taking a few seconds to scope out your immediate surroundings—even if you're someplace you've been a thousand times before.

When you're entering your workplace, school, or other familiar sites, you should already know where the exits are, and you'll also have great situational awareness about what's "normal" for that space. This could help you identify abnormalities and potential threats. But you're actually in more danger in a familiar setting than an unfamiliar one. Why? Because comfort breeds complacency, and when we get a little too comfortable, we tend to let our guard down. Don't!

If you see a suspicious or unattended bag . . .

Suspicious or unattended bags should be taken seriously, especially in public places like airports, train stations, or shopping areas.

- **DON'T TOUCH OR MOVE THE BAG.** Don't try to open, move, or inspect the bag yourself. It could be dangerous, and handling it might trigger an alarm or worse.

- **KEEP A SAFE DISTANCE.** Move away from the bag to a safe distance, ideally at least fifty to one hundred feet.

- **CALL THE POLICE.** Call 911 to report the bag. Offer as much detail as possible, including the location, a description, and any unusual circumstances (for example, if it's been unattended for a long time or seems out of place). If you see a security guard or officer nearby, tell them directly.

- **STAY CALM.** Keep calm, stay alert, and be mindful of your surroundings. Don't panic.

- **WARN PEOPLE (IF IT'S SAFE TO DO).** If you're in a busy area and it's safe to do so, discreetly inform others around you about the suspicious bag so they'll know to keep their distance.

Familiarize Yourself with the Sound of Gunfire

When a shooting breaks out, the first sound you'll probably hear is a "pop, pop, pop." This noise can be so disorienting that you might confuse it with fireworks or even a car backfiring. If you're not sure what gunfire sounds like, now's the time to change that. Take a moment to head to YouTube and listen to videos of gunshots (both indoors and outdoors) so you'll be able to recognize the sound immediately if something like this happens near you. In a moment of chaos, your ability to identify the sound of gunfire could help you stay clear-headed and avoid wasting precious time.

Run, Hide, or Fight

The FBI's official advice in an active shooter situation is simple: Run, hide, or fight. When you're faced with something so frightening, my best advice is to listen to your instincts and stay flexible. Your choice between trying to flee, taking cover, or staying put and trying to disarm the attacker depends on several factors, such as how close you are to the shooter, the overall environment, and your individual abilities. *The most important thing is to survive.* Try to keep a level head. Take whatever action makes the most sense in the moment. There are no "wrong" answers in a situation like this; your number one priority is doing what it takes to get out alive, and that means you'll likely need to improvise in a rapidly changing situation.

Run, if Possible, but Don't Blindly Follow the Crowd

Escaping the mayhem is always your top priority. As you're planning your escape, look for emergency exits, large windows, or other escape routes—not just the main doors. If there's a clear escape route and you're not in the direct line of fire, your best bet is to run as quickly and quietly as possible to safety. As previously discussed, distance is your friend; the farther you get from the attacker, the better. Do not waste time grabbing your stuff; just go.

But here's something important to remember: Don't necessarily follow the crowd. The sound of gunfire can get confusing, especially indoors, and if the noise is echoing, people might panic and start running in the wrong direction, toward the shooter. If that happens, or if you're unclear where the gunfire is coming from, don't blindly follow the pack. Try to determine where the gunfire is originating. It might be tempting to follow the herd, but staying calm and going your own way (if needed) could save your life.

Act Quickly

If you can, try to help others escape with you, but don't hesitate to leave if no one else is moving. Never wait for others to act! Once you've safely evacuated, call 911 as soon as you can.

If Escape Is Not Possible, Hide Silently

If escape is not an option, the next best course of action is to hide as quietly and discreetly as possible. When seeking safety, your options will be either to find cover or to conceal yourself.

- **COVER** provides physical protection from threats, including bullets. Examples of cover include concrete walls, large trees, or the engine compartment of a car. These barriers can stop or deflect incoming gunfire. Taking cover is your better choice.

- **CONCEALMENT** hides you from view but does not provide physical protection. If you cannot find cover, concealment may be effective in keeping you hidden from danger.

What to Do When You Call 911

When you call or text 911 to report an active shooter, make sure to provide the following critical information:

- The location of the shooting
- The number of shooters
- A physical description of the shooter(s)
- The number of victims you can see, and how many need medical help
- The type(s) of weapons

How to Text 911

If you find yourself in a dangerous situation and it's safer to text rather than call 911, here's what you need to do: Open your texting app and enter "911" in the "To" field. In the body of the text, clearly state the type of emergency and your location. If you're inside a building, include the specifics—like "second floor" or "room 314" or "library." Avoid using slang like "OMG" or "BRB." Keep it simple, direct, and concise. An agent should respond quickly to your message. While calling may seem quicker or more reliable, some critical situations require silence for survival, making texting your only viable option.

NOTE. Texting 911 is not an option in all counties or states. Knowing this in advance could save lives.

If you are indoors and unable to leave, barricade yourself in a room, lock the door if possible, and turn off the lights. If you can, choose a room with thick walls and minimal windows. If windows are present and they have blinds or curtains, pull them down to obstruct visibility from the outside. Stay as quiet as possible. Silence your phone and ensure it doesn't vibrate. Even small noises could reveal your location. If possible, position yourself strategically, so you can observe the area without being seen. This vantage point may give you the element of surprise should you need to act defensively.

If You're Forced to Fight, Anything Can Be a Weapon

Fighting should always be a last resort, done only if your life is in immediate danger. But if you have no choice, use whatever is within reach as a weapon. In this situation, there are no rules. Fight to survive. Think fast and act with as much aggression as possible. If there's a heavy object nearby—whether it's a chair, a fire extinguisher, a shovel, or a heavy backpack—use it to your advantage. You don't need a dedicated weapon to fight back; you just need to be resourceful and fierce.

If you're in a crowd (even a small one), work together to increase your chances of overpowering the attacker. Team up to ambush the assailant and use the element of surprise to your advantage. One person could focus on disarming the shooter, while another attacks their eyes and a third attempts to restrain or overpower them. The more people working together, the better your odds of survival.

If you're carrying a concealed weapon and decide to stay and fight, be aware that law enforcement may not be able to identify the "good guy" from the "bad guy." So if you're planning to fight, make sure your weapon is not in your hand when the police arrive. You don't want to be mistaken for the shooter.

In an Active School Shooting

If you find yourself in a classroom during a school shooting, time is of the essence. You may not know exactly where the shooter is or how much time you have before they arrive at your location.

If it's safe to do so, call or text the police with any information you can provide about what's going on so they can get to the scene as quickly as possible (see page 188).

If you're inside a classroom, you can try one of two approaches. The first is to try to make the room appear empty (which I call the "lights out, no one's home" approach). If it's possible to do so, putting up a sign on the door that says "class is meeting outside today" could give the impression that no one is in the room. Lock the door and turn off the lights.

Make sure all phones and watches in the room are dark and silent, with no vibrations.

The second approach is barricading the door, which can buy you precious time. If your door opens inward, use desks, chairs, or anything heavy to build a long lever that starts from right behind the door and leads all the way to a back wall. This makes it nearly impossible to physically open the door. If your door opens outward, the approach is slightly different; instead of building out, you'll build up. Your goal is that, if the shooter gets the door open, they're met with a tall barricade of desks and bookshelves that makes it hard to enter or even see anyone inside the room.

If your door opens inward, build a barricade all the way to the back wall.

If your door opens outward, build a tall barricade.

Look for improvised weapons—like a fire extinguisher that can temporarily blind the shooter if you spray it (it could also be used as a blunt force object to hit them with). You can also create a makeshift bulletproof vest by loading a backpack with heavy books and wearing it on your chest. There are also lightweight bulletproof inserts you can put into a child's backpack that can absorb or slow the impact of a bullet, reducing the likelihood of injury (see page 208). I have one in my diaper bag so if, God forbid, we found ourselves in a mass shooting event, I always have a shield I can use for my son.

Keep Your Kids Inconspicuous

For parents with younger kids, be careful about sending your children to school with light-up shoes or anything that would make them more visible in a chaotic situation. These items might draw the attention of an attacker, and in a mass shooting situation, we want to do everything possible to keep our kids inconspicuous.

In a School Bathroom or Hallway

If you're in a bathroom or hallway, your first goal should be to either get to the nearest classroom or escape the building entirely. Don't worry about trying to make it back to your specific classroom; your main priority is simply getting to safety. If you can't immediately leave the room, look for a janitor's closet or another hidden space of some kind. Also check out the windows—are any of them accessible and large enough to escape through?

You're in survival mode, so be resourceful. Could you use something from your backpack to block the door or tie it shut? Is there a huge trash can you could hide yourself in? Is there an object in the room you could use to jam the door or slow the shooter down? Think creatively and use whatever you have nearby to help yourself stay safe.

A Creative Defense Strategy

When I was in school, we would do Code Red drills (now known as active shooter drills). I was so terrified by the thought of getting stuck in the bathroom during an active shooting that I began thinking of strategies for what to do if I were ever caught in that situation. This idea is something I thought of, and it's a "thinking outside the box" strategy that could potentially help if you're stuck in a bathroom (or potentially help deter the shooter from entering the bathroom you're hiding in). Remember: Floors are slippery when wet. If you can cause a sink or toilet to overflow, do so. You can use paper towels, toilet paper rolls, or an article of clothing to clog the drain. The goal here is twofold: to create the illusion that the bathroom was evacuated in a hurry and to set up a kind of booby trap. The shooter may decide not to risk entering for fear of slipping and falling, but should they enter, they might actually slip and fall, resulting in injury.

Also, teachers (depending on your school's bathroom doors): It's not a bad idea to use a rubber door stop as your bathroom pass. This can be wedged under the door in the event that a student gets caught in the bathroom during a shooting, making the door difficult to open.

When Law Enforcement Arrives

When first responders arrive, stay calm and listen to their instructions. Don't make any sudden movements or try to approach them. Always keep your hands visible and raise them if instructed. Don't panic or yell—just follow orders. Officers may not immediately tend to the injured, as they'll be focusing on securing the area. The situation will feel chaotic, but remember that law enforcement is trained for this and will handle it in waves, from different angles.

Take your time before opening any doors. Police will announce themselves, often loudly, but it's okay to double-check. Don't feel pressured to open the door(s) immediately; your safety comes first.

Ask for verification. If you're able, call 911 and ask the dispatcher to confirm that officers are outside your door.

Discreetly look for visible identification. Through a window or peephole, check for uniforms, badges, and tactical gear. But remember, appearances alone might not guarantee safety, so trust your instincts.

Wait for clear instructions. Law enforcement will often move in groups and provide detailed directions for innocent civilians to evacuate. Follow their lead when you feel confident it's safe.

It's okay to feel nervous about waiting or verifying—police understand that these situations are terrifying. If you're ever unsure, stay hidden and secure. Trust that they would rather you take extra precautions than risk your safety or anyone else's.

After the Violence

First, if you're in this situation, let me say this: You are *not* alone in your fear, and nothing about what you're feeling is wrong.

Surviving something like this is inconceivably traumatic, and it's okay to feel disoriented, anxious, or completely unsure about what to do. Let's walk through this with a mindset of caution and care.

Once the immediate danger is over, the aftermath is its own battle. Your sense of safety may feel shattered—this is natural. You might experience waves of emotions: relief, guilt for surviving, anger, unease, or a deep sense of sadness. You might feel like life will never return to "normal," and honestly, it might not for a while. This isn't a sign of weakness—it's your body and mind processing something unimaginable.

You may find it hard to sleep, or you might feel hyperaware of your surroundings. These responses are normal; they're your brain's way of trying to protect you after trauma. Know that you don't have to go through this alone. There are therapists, support groups for those suffering from post-traumatic stress disorder, and online resources that can help you start to heal.

It takes courage to reach out for help, but you deserve support. Healing isn't linear, and there's no timeline for when you'll feel "okay" again. Remember—your feelings are valid and your survival is enough. You are not alone in this; there is a community of people ready to help you take the next step.

➤

In a mass violence situation, your primary focus is to survive—and to do *whatever* it takes to do so. Trust your instincts, do your best to stay calm, and act as quickly and safely as possible. Every second matters.

Conclusion

You can't change the past and you can't predict the future, but you can live confident, empowered, and aware. So much of life can feel out of our control—sometimes it's just being in the wrong place at the wrong time or crossing paths with the wrong person. While we may not always have control over what comes our way, we can educate ourselves, sharpen our instincts, build our strength, and prepare for life's unforeseeable moments. My hope is that this book will become a powerful resource to help you cultivate that confidence, giving you street smarts that will serve you for the rest of your life.

I'll let you in on a little secret: It's never too early *or* too late to build these instincts, to become more aware, and to protect yourself and those around you.

Street smarts isn't necessarily an innate skill, but the good news is that it's something you can develop, refine, and own. It's about trusting yourself, reading situations clearly, and knowing how to respond with confidence. It's a skill that grows with every new experience and every lesson learned. And it's one that can be passed down for generations to come.

In my eyes, there's no life skill more essential than street smarts. It's not about living scared—it's about living with a strong sense of self and an unshakable awareness of your surroundings, especially for women. This skill is a way to take back control in a world that sometimes feels tilted against us.

Should it be this way? No, of course not. But the fact of the matter is that no man will ever be able to fully understand what it feels like to move through the world as a woman. He won't know the feeling of walking through a dimly lit parking lot alone, scanning the shadows and wondering who might be watching or if danger might be lurking around the next corner. He won't experience the instinctive dread that hits when you're isolated in an elevator or a room with a stranger and something just doesn't feel right—that gut sense that makes your stomach churn and the hair on the back of your neck stand up.

It's not about paranoia—it's about survival. It's a sense of vigilance that women are forced to carry because we know all too well the dangers that exist. While many men may be supportive, kind, and empathetic, there's a layer of understanding they simply will never be able to share because they will never know what it's like to live with the constant need to assess and reassess their own safety.

My hope is that after reading this book, you feel empowered with knowledge. I want you to lean into the power of awareness, tap into your intuition, and refuse to shrink back. I want you to carry this confidence forward, knowing that with each step, you're living a life that's bold, aware, and unmistakably strong.

Always remember:

- A distracted person is an easy target.

- In a scary situation, noise and distance are your friends.

- If something feels off, you're probably right—trust your gut.

- Never be embarrassed to ask for help or call 911.

- Choose de-escalation over confrontation.

- Situational awareness is your best first line of defense.

- Lie to survive.

- And most importantly—live aware, not in fear.

Acknowledgments

Thank you to my son—my beautiful, brilliant, brave, curious, strong, sweet, wild, and lovable little boy. You are my world, my inspiration, and my heart that beats outside of my body. You teach me every day what it means to love so purely, to see the world with wonder, and to live with courage and kindness. I am so proud of the person you are and the incredible person I know you're becoming. Always be true to yourself, dream big, and know that, no matter what, I will always be your biggest fan and your safest place. I love you more than words could ever express and will forever be in your corner, cheering you on through every chapter of life. You are my everything, now and forever.

My husband—thank you for loving me exactly as I am and for always encouraging me to embrace my true self and go after my dreams, no matter how big, insane, or wild they may seem. Your belief in me gives me strength, and your support makes me feel like I can take on anything. I'm so lucky to love and be loved by you, to laugh with you until it hurts, to weather the hard moments with you by my side, and to share this beautifully messy life together. You're my partner, and my forever.

Dad—since I was a little girl, you've been my rock, my confidant, and my best friend. You've always had my back, no matter what, and believed in me even when I didn't believe in myself. You made me the strong, confident woman I am today and taught me to stand up for what I believe in and to fight for what's right, no matter how hard it may be. I admire and look up to you for so many reasons—your strength, your knowledge, your wisdom, and the way you've always shown up for me and the people you love are just a few. You've been my biggest supporter and the foundation I've built so much of my life on. I'll always be so incredibly proud to be your little girl, and I hope you know how much I love you and how grateful I am to call you my daddio. You mean the world to me, always and forever.

Mom—you nurtured my innate gift of street smarts and taught me how to see the world clearly, to trust my instincts, and to be prepared for the real dangers that exist. You've always had this way of balancing protection with independence, letting me grow while always being there to catch me when I fell. You've shown me the meaning of unconditional love in everything you do. You stood by my side, cheering me on during the highs, and you picked me up with the perfect words when I needed them most. You're my best friend, my safe haven, and the reason I hold myself to such a high standard. I always want to make you proud. I love you more.

Fitz and Frank—my little fur babies who bring me so much love and joy (and of course craziness, which I wouldn't have any other way). Your beautiful hearts are selfless, endless, and a living testament to the power of unwavering love and loyalty. Your quiet devotion is untouched by time or circumstance and your existence is a true gift to my life. I love you, Fitzy bug and Frankie boy.

My family—thank you for being the foundation of so much good in my life. You're the people I will always hold near and dear, and I cherish every single memory we've made together, especially the moments filled with fun, silliness, and laughter. We share an unbreakable bond that makes us who we are. Our closeness has been my constant, a source of strength and comfort that I've leaned on more than you know. I'll forever be grateful for the love we share and the unbreakable bond that ties us together. You mean so much to me, and I feel so lucky to call you mine.

This book would not have been possible without my incredible dream team of powerhouse women. From the very beginning, I dreamed of working with a team who not only believed in my vision but also brought it to life with passion, talent, and heart. To my dream team, each of you has exceeded every expectation. You've made this process not only possible but genuinely enjoyable, too, and I feel so lucky to have been surrounded by such inspiring, supportive, strong, badass, and driven women who share in the purpose of this project. Together, we've turned an idea into something meaningful, incredibly impactful, and evergreen. I couldn't be more grateful.

Claire Harris—my agent, whom I will forever be deeply grateful for. From our very first call, I knew we'd clicked in a way that felt easy, rare, and special. Your belief in me and my purpose has been nothing short of inspiring, and the way you've guided, supported, and advocated for me has meant the world to me. You are so much more than an agent—you are a loyal friend and a steady light helping me navigate this incredible journey, which has been a dream come true. Thank you for being someone I know I can trust wholeheartedly. Thank you for being you.

Laura Barcella—my right-hand woman. Working with you has been such a joy. From the moment we started, I felt like I could just be myself, and your energy, creativity, and thoughtfulness have been everything I could have hoped for and more. I am so grateful for the countless hours on the phone to brainstorm, laugh, and help keep me on track. So many times I felt as if we shared the same brain. This book wouldn't have been possible without you by my side. Thank you for making what seemed like a daunting process so fun and smooth. You are amazing, and I am so lucky to have you.

Cassie Jones—my wonderful editor. From the very beginning, I knew I wanted *you* to be the one to help bring this dream to life, and I can't tell you how lucky I feel that it all worked out. You saw my vision right away and ran with it in a way that feels almost magical. Your kindness, support, and belief in this project has meant so much to me. You've inspired me throughout this process, and your ability to not only see my goal but also elevate it to something even greater is truly remarkable. Thank you for pouring so much of yourself into this and for making this dream a reality. I'm beyond grateful to get to do this with you and can't wait to see the impact this book will have on so many.

The team at William Morrow/HarperCollins—especially Tess Day, Melissa Esner, Mark Robinson, Rachel Meyers, Elina Cohen and Andrew DiCecco—thank you for believing in this project and for the care, creativity, and intention you've brought to every part of this process. It's been such a gift to work alongside a team who values the heart behind the words and worked so hard to shape this book into what it is. A special thank-you to Nicole Braun—Cassie's right-hand woman. Nicole, your kindness, organization, and attention to detail has made all the difference. I'm so grateful for the many ways you helped bring this project together.

To my brilliant illustrator, Alexis Seabrook—what an absolute dream it's been to collaborate with you. From the very beginning, you understood the heart of this project and approached every detail with creativity, care, and a clear, artistic vision. Your ability to take an idea and transform it into something vibrant and meaningful is truly remarkable. But beyond your immense talent, you've been a joy to work with—kind, thoughtful, collaborative, and just the sweetest human. You've made this process so fun and easy, and your work is such an important and beautiful part of this book. I'm forever grateful to have you on this team and couldn't imagine this book without your art woven throughout.

A heartfelt thank-you to my incredibly talented photographer, Anna Gunselman. You were an absolute bright light to work with. You brought so much kindness, warmth, creativity, and vision to every moment—and saw me for me. You captured me in a way that felt empowering and honest, and made me feel at ease in a space that doesn't always come naturally to me. Anna, you are such a gift. I'm so grateful our paths crossed, and even more grateful you were part of this project.

A List of Safety Tools

The choice of self-defense tool (or tools) is a deeply personal decision, and I strongly encourage you to carry what you feel most comfortable with while also ensuring you are educated on and trained with your chosen device. There are various options available, ranging from lethal to nonlethal, and it's ultimately up to you to determine what aligns with your comfort level and personal safety preferences. The tools described below are nonlethal in nature, and while I provide these options for consideration, the final decision rests with you. Please ensure that any tool you choose is used responsibly, with proper training, and in accordance with your local laws.

Anti-Choking Device

An anti-choking device is a lifesaving tool designed to help in situations where traditional methods like the Heimlich maneuver aren't possible. It's a mask that fits over the person's mouth and nose. There are two sizes: one for adults and one for children. When you pull the handle, it creates a strong vacuum suction that helps dislodge the object blocking the airway, giving the person a chance to breathe again.

Bulletproof Plate

This is a lightweight, flexible plate insert designed to be slipped into a child's backpack, a purse, or a diaper bag for added protection in the event of a school shooting or similar emergency. Made from bullet-resistant materials, it absorbs the bullet's energy before it can enter the body, offering peace of mind without adding much bulk or weight.

Car Escape Tool

This small but powerful tool is designed to help you escape your car if you're ever trapped inside—whether from a crash or because the vehicle is sinking in water. It includes a window breaker, which is either a spring-loaded device that shatters tempered glass instantly with a push, or a hammer-like tool that you swing to break the glass. This tool also typically includes a seat belt cutter, which is a razor-sharp blade that slices through a jammed seat belt in seconds, giving you a way out when every second counts.

Door Security Bar

This is a simple but effective way to keep a door from being forced open. You can use it on a regular hotel room door or sliding glass door to amp up your security. The adjustable bar fits under the door handle and against the floor, making it harder for someone to break in. Some bars even have a built-in alarm that goes off as a result of the pressure/vibration caused when someone tries to open the door. You can also use these bars on windows that open up or down or slide left to right. See page 131 for more information.

Doorstop Alarm

This device blocks a door from opening while also sounding a loud, jarring alarm if someone tries to force their way in. It's an easy-to-use, battery-powered tool that fits like a doorstop at the base of the door. If anyone attempts to open the door, the alarm goes off, scaring off intruders and alerting others to your situation. See page 130 for more information.

Hair-Tie Drink Cover

This clever tool is a discreet and easy way to protect your drink from being tampered with when you're out. It looks like a regular scrunchie but has a hidden stretchy cover that you can pull over the top of your drink. It's simple, portable, and gives you added peace of mind when you're out and about.

Pepper Gel / Pepper Spray

Pepper gel and pepper spray are both designed to incapacitate an attacker by irritating their eyes, skin, and respiratory system, but they work differently. Pepper spray uses a cloud-like mist that covers a wide area. It's good for close-range use, but it carries the risk of blowback toward you, especially outside. Pepper gel is thicker and stickier, making it more precise and better for longer distances. It also has less risk of blowback. If you need to use pepper gel or spray, aim for the attacker's eyes, nose, and mouth. The goal is to disable the attacker long enough for you to escape safely.

Personal Key Chain Alarm

This is one of the easiest self-defense tools to carry because it's small, lightweight, and requires no skill or strength to use. Most personal key chain alarms have a pull tab or button that when activated blasts a loud, high-pitched siren. This is meant to shock and disorient an attacker while drawing attention from those around you, giving you a chance to escape or get help.

Portable Steel Door Lock

These small, inexpensive locks offer added protection by preventing your door from being opened—even if someone has a key. They hook onto the strike plate on the doorframe and lock into place manually when you close the door. While I'd recommend using a door security bar or doorstop alarm for easier removal in case of fire, this lock can bring extra peace of mind for adjoining hotel room doors or when staying in places with questionable door security. See page 131 for more information.

Stun Gun

This compact, portable self-defense tool delivers an electric shock to temporarily disable an attacker. With a simple trigger, it sends a high-voltage charge that disrupts their nervous system, causing pain and muscle weakness, which will give you the chance to escape. It's small enough to fit in your hand or purse, offering a smart and effective way to stay safe. It's primarily a last-resort option—as always, your first goal is to avoid a physical confrontation.

Tactical Pen

This discreet self-defense tool looks like an ordinary pen, but it's built with durable materials and often includes features like a pointed end for self-defense, a built-in flashlight, or even a tempered glass breaker. You can carry it daily without anyone noticing, and it could be a lifesaver if you ever need to protect yourself or escape from a dangerous situation. This is the tool for you if you're trained in hand-to-hand combat. It should be used only as a last resort, when keeping your distance is not possible.

Travel Carbon Monoxide Detector

This small portable device alerts you if there's dangerous carbon monoxide gas in the air—which you can't see, smell, or taste. It constantly monitors the air and will sound an alarm if the levels become unsafe, warning you to immediately leave the building. It's a must-have when traveling.

Index

A

Accessories, flashy, 72
Acquaintance stalker, 67–69
Active school shootings, 190–95
Active shooter drills, 194
Airbags, 54
AirTag, 111
Air travel, 122–24
Alarm systems, 102
Alcala, Rodney, 27
Alcohol, excessive, 74–75, 154
Alerts, enabling, 177
Aliases, 109, 162
Angel shot, 19
Anxiety, managing, 94
Apple Pay, 38
Armed robberies, 29
Arrested, while traveling, 139
Arrogance, 66
Artificial intelligence (AI), 168–70
ATM withdrawals, 109–10
Attachments, in emails and texts, 163–64
Authority, false, 9

B

Babysitting, 98–99
Baggage, while traveling, 118
Bags, suspicious or unattended, 185
Banking online, 168
Bank scams, 167
Bars or clubs, 7, 18–19
Barth, Charles "Chuck," xi
Barzee, Wanda, 29
Bathroom buddy, 77
Bathrooms or hallways
  handbags in, 77, 123
  in schools, 193–94
Beaches, 125, 133–36
Behavioral warning signs, 5–9
Being followed or watched
  in elevators, 21–22, 121
  in parking lot or garage, 27–28, 55, 56–57, 91–92
  stalkers, 67–69, 94–95
  in a store, 137–38
  traveling alone, 120
  while driving, 40

Being followed or watched (*cont.*)
    to and from work, 91–92
    to your home, 113–14
    to your hotel, 128
Blackmail, 170
Blind spots, 41–42
Bosses, discomfort around, 93–94
Boundary pushing, 6
Bragging, 66
Breast pumps, 95
Bulletproof vest, makeshift, 192
Bundy, Ted, 8–9, 78
Burner numbers, 129

C

Campus gym, 152–53
Captive, being held, 20
Carbon monoxide detector, 132
Car doors, locking
    after fender bender, 39
    at car wash, 36
    at gas stations, 37
    at home, 35, 44
    at parking lots, 91
    when driving, 40, 53
Car escape tools, 132, 155
Cars. *See also* Driving
    break-ins, 53–54
    bumper stickers or decals, 53
    carjacking, 38–39
    keeping feet on the floor, 54
    personal items in, 53–54, 122
    unmarked, 37
    using as a barrier, 36, 55–56
    when trouble strikes, 46–52
Car seats, by roadside, 39
Cash, from ATMs, 109–10
Catcalls, 136–37
Cell phones
    burner numbers, 129
    charger safety, 132, 178

    and driving, 33–35
    emergency SOS function, 114
    keeping fully charged, 148
    and kids, 44
    location services, 172
    location sharing, 119, 148
    not giving out number, 62
    out of service range, 51
Chargers, public, 132, 178
Charging-only cable, 178
Charity scams, 168
Charm, excessive, 5
ChatGPT, 169
Check-in person, 71–72, 104
Children
    and babysitters, 98–99
    keeping inconspicuous, 193
    posting photos of, 173
    teaching about traffic and cars, 43–44
Child safety course, 98
Clutter, 87
Code Red drills, 194
Code words, 76
Coffee shops, 17–18
College life
    freshman year, 145–46
    going-out guidelines, 153–56
    mental health, 156–57
    not revealing where you live, 22
    the red zone, 144–45
    safety precautions, 147–53
Computers, at work, 89. *See also* Digital safety
Counselors, 95
Credit cards, 38
Crimes
    least ideal targets, 119–20
    men against women, 2–3
    sexual assault, 2, 15, 144
    statistics on, 2
Crises, manufactured, 8–9

INDEX 215

Crosswalks, 44
Customer stalkers, 94–95
Cybercriminals, 163

D

Data harvesting, 164
Dating safely
    first-date safety, 59–62
    online and app dating, 63–67
    stalkers, 67–69
Dating scams, 165, 169
Deep fakes, 169
De-escalation tactics, 96
Delivery drivers, 106
Delivery people, 107
Denial, danger of, 3
Designated driver, 73–74
Designated sober friend, 73–74, 154–55
Desk drawers, locking, 88
Detainees, 139
Digital safety, 159–79. *See also* Social media
    AI and internet fraud, 164, 168–70
    assessing legitimacy of emails or texts, 162–63
    banking online, 168
    clicking links in emails or texts, 163–64
    common online scams, 165–68
    digital footprint, 160
    "fun" online quizzes, 176
    layers of defense, 176–79
    passwords, 161–62
    phone location services, 172
    revenge porn or sextortion, 170–71
    RFID blocking, 179
    scams, statistics on, 161
    separate email accounts, 162
    unknown websites, 164
    using Google, 173–75
    on work computer, 89
Domestic violence, 20, 29
"Do Not Disturb Sign" trick, 127
Door attendants, 109
Doorbell camera, 102
Doors
    barricading, 191–92
    locking, 101–2, 131, 149
    and strangers, 106–7
Doorstop alarm, 130, 149
Dorm entrances, 147–48
Dorm safety, 147–49
Dowel rods, 103
Dreams, 10–11
Drinks, watching carefully, 61–62, 73
Driving
    behind trucks with large loads, 43
    being followed while, 40
    blind spots, 41–42
    car emergency items, 52
    carjack attempts, 38–39
    car trouble, 46–52
    distracted, 33–35, 51
    fender-bender con, 39
    forgetting where you parked, 56–57
    getting gas safely, 37–38
    home garage safety, 35–36
    keeping feet on the car floor, 54
    leaving yourself an "out," 39
    left-turn rule, 40–41
    parent PSAs, 43–44
    parking lot safety, 54–56
    personal identification items in car, 53–54, 122
    road rage, 45–46
    two-second rule, 45
    unmarked cars, 37
    what not to do, 35
    to work and back, 91–92

Drugged, acting, 77–78
Drugs, 153–54

E

Electric shocks, 47–50
Electric vehicles, 38
Elevator safety, 21–22, 121
Email
    clicking links in, 163–64
    determining legitimacy of, 162–63
    personal, 89
    separate, for different purposes, 162
Emergency code word, 76
Emergency exits, 87
Emergency items for car, 52
Emergency phones on campus, 147
Emotional burnout, 95–96
Encryption, 178
Escape routes, 40, 186–87
Escort systems on campus, 147
Exercising safely, 30, 110–11

F

Face recognition, disabling, 173–74
False assurances, 6
False vulnerability, 8–9
Fast-tracking relationships, 6
Fawn response, 26
Fear and intimidation, 8
Federal Bureau of Investigation (FBI)
    advice on active shooter situations, 186
    careers in the, xi–xii
    Internet Crime Complaint Center, 165
Federal Trade Commission, 165
Fender-bender con, 39
Fighting, in active shooter situation, 189–90

Fight mode, 24–25
Financial institutions, 168
Fire and safety drills, 87
Fire extinguishers, 87, 192
Firing someone, 96–98
First-aid equipment, 87–88
First dates, 59–62
Flags, safety, 133–34
Flares, 51
Flashy accessories, 72
Flight mode, 25
Flipping a switch in behavior, 9
Fraud, internet, 164, 168–70
"Free gift" messages, 167
Freeze mode, 25–26
Freshman year, 145–46
Friends. *See also* Going out with friends
    bathroom buddy, 77
    at college, 145–46, 153–56
    designated sober, 73–74, 154–55
    made on vacation, 129–30
    "messy," 74–75
Front blind spot, 41
"Fun" online quizzes, 176

G

Garage opener key chain, 35–36
Garage opener remotes, 35
Garages, at home, 35–36, 102
Garbage, 103–4
Gaslighting, 8
Gas stations, 37–38
Generative AI, 169
Gestures, secret, 76
Girl codes, 76
Going out with friends
    at college, 153–56
    hailing rideshare or taxi, 81–83
    safety story, 80–81
    tips for, 71–80

Google
  Alerts, 174–75
  Maps, 175
  Photos, 173
  Street View, 175
  using wisely, 173–75
GPS, 34, 36, 122
Gravel trucks, 43
Grocery shopping, 55–56
Grooming for exploitation, 8
Gunfire, 186, 187
Gut feelings. *See* Intuition
Gyms, on campus, 152–53

H

Hallways or bathrooms, 193–94
Handbags
  fancy, leaving at home, 72
  hanging on bathroom door, 77, 123
  at workplace, 88
Hand signal for help, 31
Harassment, 92–93, 136–37
Hazard lights, 39
Help, unsolicited, 8
Hiding silently, 187–89
Highland Park, IL, xii–xiii
Home address, 109, 122
Home break-ins or invasions
  real-life story, 105
  scripting it out, 107
  what to do, 114–15
Home security systems, 69
Hostage situations, 29
Hotels
  abuser or attacker in, 20
  being followed back to, 128
  real-world safety story, 121
  safety tips, 126–29
Hotel transportation, 124
House keys, 103

"https" with lock symbol, 164
Human Resources (HR), 94, 96
Human trafficking, 29–30

I

Indoor cameras, 98
Instacart, 107
Instagram, 173
Insult manipulation, 6
International airports, 123–24
Internet. *See* Digital safety
"Interview" questions, 5–6
Intimidation and fear, 8
Intuition
  analyzing dreams, 10–11
  behavioral warning signs, 5–9
  decoding red flags, 5
  psychology behind, 3–4
  as survival instinct, 3–4
  trusting, 4, 79, 182
Isolation from support system, 8, 66
Itinerary, sharing, 118–19

J

Jewelry, 72
Job offers, fake, 167
Juice jacking, 178
Jungle juice, 154

K

Keys, spare, 103

L

Language translator app, 124
Las Vegas Strip, 181
Laundry facilities, 152–53
Law enforcement, 195. *See also* Police
Left-side blind spot, 42

Left-turn rule, 40–41
Letting someone go, 96–98
Lie to survive
　common scenarios, 17–22
　to get out of a date, 67
　getting over "lying isn't nice," 15–16
　origin story behind, 13–14
　playing along as only option, 26–30
　referring to boyfriend or husband, 17–22
　with taxi or rideshare driver, 82
　when "No" is not accepted, 24–26
　when traveling, 23
Lighting, and safety, 80, 102
Links, in texts and emails, 163–64
Living alone
　never open your door to strangers, 106–7
　real-world safety story, 105, 108
　safety tips, 101–5, 107, 109–11, 113–15
　selecting a roommate, 112–13
　setting up a strong (safe) room, 114
Location services, 172
Location sharing, 119, 148
Lottery scams, 166–67
Love-bombing, 66, 165
Luggage, 118

M

Mail and packages, 104
Malware, 163, 164
Mass violence
　active school shootings, 190–95
　after the violence, 195–96
　run, hide, or fight responses, 186–90
　sounds of gunfire, 186
　ten-second rule, 184–85
　warning signs, 183–84
Men
　crimes against women, 2–3
　as "faux boyfriends," 16
　as faux male "roommates," 109
　how they talk about women, 65
　rape offenders, 2
　street harassment, 136–37
Mental health
　after mass violence, 195–96
　at college, 156–57
　and work, 95–96
"Messy" friends, 74–75
Mitchell, Brian David, 29
Motion-sensor cameras, 102
Multifactor authentication (MFA), 176–77

N

Name tags, 94
Neighborhood crime, 104
Neighbors, 103
Night classes, 150–51
911
　calling, to verify police officers, 37, 195
　discreetly asking for help, 20–21
　how to text, 188–89
　reporting an active shooter, 188
"No," learning to say, 7, 24, 96
Nursing mothers, 95

O

Office. *See also* Workplace
　badges, 89–90
　doors, locking, 88
　layout and exits, 87
　networks, 89

Online and app dating, 63–67
Online dating profiles, 64–66
Online quizzes, 176
Orlando nightclub massacre, 181

P

Package delivery scams, 167
Packages and mail, 104
Parents, vehicle PSAs for, 43–44
Parking garages and lots
    at airports, 122
    escaping danger at, 27–28, 56–57, 90–91
    safety tips, 54–55, 122
    varying where you park, 91
Parties, 154
Passenger seat, 54
Passports, 123, 139
Password manager, 162
Passwords, online, 161–62
Pepper gel or spray
    in checked luggage, 132
    on dates, 61
    how to use, 63
    in ridesharing situation, 155
    when going out with friends, 72
    when traveling alone, 114
Perpetrators, warning signs of, 183–84
Personal information
    aliases instead of real name, 94, 109
    and cybercriminals, 163–64, 166
    Google Alert for, 174–75
    hiding, in or on cars, 53–54, 122
    home address, 109, 122
    on items in your trash, 104
    and online banking, 168
    oversharing, at office, 86–87
    oversharing, on first date, 62
    phishing scams, 163, 165–66, 169
    phone number, 62
    on social media, 76, 160
    and traveling solo, 126, 129–30
    in workplace, 88, 89
Personal key chain alarm, 72, 132
Personal life, boundaries around, 62, 86–87
Pets, 44
Phishing scams
    about, 165–66
    and generative AI, 169
    signs of, 163
Pickpockets, 119
Pink cocaine, 153–54
Pizza ordering, on 911 calls, 20
Playing along to survive, 26–30
Police, 37, 195
Porn, revenge, 170–71
Portable steel door lock, 131
Post-traumatic stress disorder, 196
Power bank, portable, 178
Power lines, fallen, 47–50
Predators and serial killers, 29, 78
Pregnancy, 95
Private transport buses, 141
Psychology behind intuition, 3–4
Public charging stations, 178
Public transport, 140–41
Purses, 88, 123

Q

Quizzes, online, 176

R

Rape offenders, 2
Real-world safety stories
    alcohol or substance consumption, 80–81
    attempted break-in, 105
    at the beach, 125

Real-world safety stories (*cont.*)
  being isolated with unsafe person, 9–10
  car washes, 36
  dates gone wrong, 69
  elevators, 121
  hotels, 121
  parking garages, 56–57
  parking lots, 27–28, 90–91
  subcontractors, 108
  walking alone, 151–52
Rear blind spot, 41
Red flags, decoding, 5
Red zone, 144–45
Reflective surfaces, 140
Resort vacations, 128–29
Revenge porn, 170–71
RFID blocking, 179
Rideshares
  escaping from car, 155–56
  not disclosing where you live, 19–20, 61
  safety guidelines, 81–83, 141, 155–56
Right-side blind spot, 42
Rip currents, 134–36
Road rage, 45–46
Road trips, 46–47
Robberies, 29, 138
Romance scams, 165, 169
Romantic stalker, 67–69
Roommates, 112–13, 146
Room service ordering, on 911 calls, 20–21
Running, in active shooter situation, 186–87
Running alone, 30, 110–11

S

Safety equipment, 87–88
Safety flags at beaches, 133–34
Safety tools for traveling, 130–32
Safety workshops, 147
Sandy Hook Elementary, 181
Satellite calling or texting, 51
Scams
  fake websites, 164
  most common online, 165–68
  phishing, 163, 165–66, 169
  statistics on, 161
School bathrooms or hallways, 193–94
School bus safety, 43
School shootings, 190–95
Scripted-out situations
  dodging stranger in campus spaces, 153
  dodging stranger when traveling alone, 23
  dodging unsolicited taxi driver, 124
  escaping stranger at bar or club, 7
  getting out of a date, 66–67
  helping "messy" friend, 74–75
  letting someone go, 97–98
  preventing a home invasion, 107
Seat belts, 34, 54
Secret gestures, 76
Security bar, 131
Security systems, 102
Self-care, 96
Self-defense classes, 147
Selfishness, 65–66
Semitrucks, 41–42
Serial killers, 29, 78
Sextortion, online, 170–71
Sexually related crimes
  on campus, 144
  statistics on, 2, 15
Sexual references, 66
Shift in behavior, sudden, 9
"Shoe Behind the Door" trick, 127
Sign for help, universal, 31

Situational awareness
    as first line of defense, 72
    looking at reflective surfaces, 140
    making it a habit, 184–85
    walking alone at night, 150
    when out with friends, 72
Skimmer devices, 38
Sliding glass doors, 102–3
Smart, Elizabeth, 29
Sober buddies, 154–55
Sober leader, 73–74
Social media
    at college, 148–49
    not posting in real time, 110, 119, 172
    privacy settings, 88–89
    profiles, 60, 64
    safety tips, 76, 172–73
Squad safety. *See* Going out with friends
Stalkers, 67–69, 94–95
Stop signs, 40
Story inconsistencies, 8
Street harassment, 136–37
Street Smart Blonde social media, xiv
Stress responses, 24–26
Strollers, by roadside, 39
Strong (or safe) room, 114
Stun gun, 156
Subcontractors, 108
Suicide prevention, 156–57
Support groups, 196
Survival, playing along for, 26–30
Sweepstakes scams, 166–67

T

Tactical pen, 132, 156
Taxis, 81–83, 124, 141
Tech support scams, 167
Ten-second rule, 184–85

Texting
    for 911 help, 188–89
    satellite, 51
    while driving, 33–35
Texts, suspicious, 162–64
Therapists, 95, 196
Touch-to-pay methods, 38
Tracking devices, 39, 111
Tradespeople, 107
Trafficking, 29–30
Traffic lights, 40, 45
Transitional spaces, 79–80
Trauma, 196
Traveling alone
    air travel, 122–24
    beach trip safety flags, 133–34
    being arrested or detained, 139
    being robbed, 138
    hotel safety, 126–29
    lying to survive, 23
    mixing and mingling, 129–30
    public transport, 140–41
    real-world safety story, 121, 125
    rip currents, 134–36
    safety tips, 118–20
    safety tools, 130–32
    scripts, 124
    street harassment, 136–38
Triangle method of grocery shopping, 55–56
Trucks, heavy, 41–42, 43
Two-second rule, 45

U

Uber Eats, 107
Ubers and Uber drivers
    not disclosing home address, 19–20, 61
    researching legitimany of, 141
Universal sign for help, 31
Universities, 22. *See also* College life

USB data blocker, 179
US Department of State, 139

V

Victim blaming, 2
Viruses, computer, 163, 164
Voice cloning, 169
VPN, 132

W

Walking alone
   after evening out, 75
   precautions to take, 110–11, 150–52
Wall outlets, 179
Weapons, improvised, 192
Websites
   checking legitimacy of, 164
   fake, 163
   tracking by, 89
   unheard of, 164
Wedding rings, 65
Well-lit locations, 79–80
Wi-Fi, public, 132
Wilder, Christopher, 28
Window-breaking tool, 155
Windows, locking
   at college, 149
   at home, 102–3
   at hotels, 126
Woman of the Hour (movie), 27
Women
   critical comments about, 65
   sexually related crimes against, 2–3, 15
   solo runs or walks, 30, 110–11
   street harassment, 136–37
Working late, 90, 92
Work-life balance, 95
Workplace
   babysitter tips, 98–99
   letting someone go, 97–98
   safety tips, 85–97
Work uniforms, 89–90